Beginner's Guide to
Family History Research

Beginner's Guide to Family History Research

Fourth Edition

By Desmond Walls Allen
and Carolyn Earle Billingsley

This special fourth edition was
published expressly for
Mindscape Software, Inc.

Published by
Research Associates
PO Box 303
Conway, AR 72033

ISBN 1-56546-128-2

Printed in the United States of America

Preface

Congratulations on deciding to learn about a fascinating hobby! Once you begin, you will find family history research interesting, intriguing and addictive. You will become a private investigator and dive into a never-ending, real life puzzle. The pieces of the puzzle will tell you who you are; who the people were who contributed to your genetic makeup; how they lived; what events shaped their lives; and why they did the things they did. We hope you'll understand more about yourself as you learn about the people who contributed to your physical and psychological make-up.

The purpose of this book is to launch you on your quest. It is written in simple terms so you, the beginner, will get a basic grasp of the subject of family history and genealogy.

What is the difference between family history and genealogy? Genealogy is the study of your direct ancestors and their families, while family history is a broader topic. It adds an historical touch to your research, an understanding of the times in which your ancestors lived.

There are two very important concepts in this book:

- *How* you know is as important as *what* you know. We have given examples for you to follow in recording *how* you know. This concept is called 'citing your sources.'

- The families with whom your ancestors associated in their business, social, religious, and extended family groups are very important to your research.

We will remind you of these concepts as we introduce you to sources of information about your ancestors.

Since we cannot tell you everything about family history research, we have included a resource section and bibliography at the end of this book, pointing you toward sources for more information.

Terms specific to genealogy and family history are listed in a glossary preceding the resource section.

Welcome!

Preface to the Fourth Edition

This, the fourth edition of *Beginner's Guide to Family History Research*, has evolved from

- our teaching experience,
- our readers' suggestions,
- recommendations from other teachers,
- and changes we saw in the field of genealogy.

We teach genealogy. Our *Beginner's Guide* is designed to be used as a textbook to supplement learning materials in a classroom setting. But it's also for the independent learners who want to jump right in and start researching their families' histories.

We didn't write this book for the masses—we wrote it with one typical researcher in mind. She's a busy careerperson with family and civic responsibilities. She can't devote large blocks of time to the pursuit of her ancestors, but she wants to get started *now*. And since her time is valuable, she wants to maximize her efforts by getting off on the right track.

We're listening to your stories about problems you're having with your research. (We've had many of those same problems ourselves.) One theme we've heard repeated many times is, "I wish I'd known to cite my sources from the very beginning." So we're encouraging you to do so. We hear "dead-end" stories from people who were successful in their problem solving only after they retraced their research steps and gathered information about the groups of people who were fellow-travelers with their ancestors.

We are still learning ourselves. We attend conferences, read journal articles and new books, and explore new information sources ourselves. We're always looking for new and better ways to trap elusive ancestors. We listen to our peers in the genealogy field—they're learning all the time, too.

The biggest change we see in genealogy and family history research is the impact of computer use. Computer software has turned the difficult organizational challenge of genealogy into an easy task.

Desmond Walls Allen
Carolyn Earle Billingsley
July 1998

Table of Contents

Is Family History for You? - 1

Why Explore Family History?

There are almost as many reasons to research your family history as there are genealogists. It's a fascinating hobby. Did you like to hear your grandmother's stories of the 'old days'? Was history one of your favorite subjects in school? Do you like to read historical novels?

Are you curious about your ancestors? Did you always wonder where your red hair or your son's left-handedness came from, or which side of the family was tall or short, or just what kind of people your ancestors were? You may be interested in these questions, as well as those of a medical nature. It may be important to you to find out whether there is a history of heart disease or cancer in your family, which might affect your health care.

You may want to discover the truth about old family legends, stories or mysteries. Are there stories in your family about your grandfather riding with Jesse James, or your great grandmother having six sets of twins? Did one of your ancestors kill a man and flee the state? Are you related to General Robert E. Lee or President John Adams or some other famous person?

You might want to join a lineage society, such as the Daughters of the American Revolution, Colonial Dames, Sons of Confederate Veterans, or Mayflower Descendants. Joining requires proving your family link to an appropriate person—a Revolutionary War soldier, a person who resided in America in Colonial times, a Confederate veteran, or someone who arrived on the *Mayflower*.

Perhaps you want to research your family history to qualify for benefits, scholarships or grants through Indian tribal membership. Or perhaps you want to prove your claim to an inheritance.

You may have a genuine interest in preserving the past, either for your children or grandchildren or simply for posterity. You may want to record the memories of older people in your community or your own recollections.

All of these are valid reasons for beginning the wonderful hobby of family history research.

Who Can Do It?

You can explore your genealogy, no matter where you live! Many successful genealogists operate entirely from their homes, writing letters and using the telephone. If you can write or type a letter or use the telephone, you can research your family history.

Eventually you may want to travel in pursuit of your new hobby. You will want to go to libraries, archives, and courthouses, and to the actual places where your great grandparents and other family members lived.

Perhaps you'll hire a professional to do all of your research, or maybe you will hire a professional occasionally to get at those records you need in other states or countries [see chapter 12]. Even if you hire a professional to do your entire family history, you should be familiar with the subjects in this book in order to communicate with the person you hire and to understand the material you receive.

Is Family History Research Expensive?

It can be as expensive as you let it be! Research can be done at little expense if you use common materials at hand, such as boxes for your files, and plain paper for recording information instead of pre-printed forms. To reduce costs, use your library's resources instead of buying expensive books. Photocopy the pages from books of interest to you. (Remember copyright restrictions!) Find out about book and microfilm rental programs and interlibrary loans.

Perhaps you won't need to hire professionals to search those out-of-state records if you're patient and order microfilms to view locally or you find people in other states or countries who are searching for the same families and can help your search.

Of course, research can be expensive, depending on your desires and circumstances. You may buy file cabinets, a computer, and many books. You can make special trips to every location of interest and travel to Europe to visit your family's ancestral home. But that's up to you.

So now that you know that you *can* trace your family, let's deal with the *how* of researching your family history.

Starting Your Search

Start with yourself! Gather records proving who you are, then do the same thing for your children and grandchildren. Work backward in time, doing the same for your parents and their parents. Continue working step by step back in time along your family lines.

Jumping back in time and skipping generations is generally a waste of time. You may be tempted to immediately skip several generations and start looking for information on your grandfather who served in the War Between the States. Yes, you might find information by skipping directly back to him in the records, but you may have difficulty finding the right person and understanding the records you've found if you haven't laid the proper groundwork.

Place names are important! As you search home and family sources, be alert for names of villages, towns, cities, counties, states, foreign countries. Write down not only the place names you encounter, but the exact sources where you learned of those place names.

Gathering Family Documents and Photographs

How do you prove who you are and who your parents and grandparents were? The first step is to gather various documents in your home and the homes of family members.

Get copies of birth certificates for every person in your family for whom they are available. There is no need to order a certified copy of each certificate, photocopies of the certificates you locate within the family will usually be sufficient.

Where to Write for Vital Records: Births, Deaths, Marriages and Divorces is an inexpensive booklet published by the US Department of Health and Human Services. It lists the name and address of each state's vital records agency, the current cost of ordering a record from that state, and the dates for which these records are available. You can also call Social Security Administration's toll-free telephone number and ask a representative about the fees and addresses to obtain vital records. (Check your telephone directory under US Government, Social Security Administration, for the number.)

Birth certificates generally show a person's date and place of birth, full name, and the parents' names, including their places of birth. While you're gathering birth certificates, get copies of all death certificates available for your family members. These show the death date, place and cause of death, place of burial, date of birth, and the parents' names (so far as the informant's information was correct).

Seek out other material relating to you or your family, such as:

- Personal papers (diaries, letters, scrapbooks)
- School records:
      Report cards
      Diplomas
      Special awards or activities
- Employment records
- Military service and discharge papers
- Newspaper clippings:
      Birth announcements
      Obituaries
      Announcements of engagement, marriage, military service, etc.
- Court documents:
      Deeds, tax records, court actions, marriage/ divorce papers
- Church Records
      Baptism, confirmation, birth, death, or burial records
- Family Bible
- Family photographs

Citing Sources

As you examine each document or photograph, remember to carefully cite the source of your information. Make a note on the back of each photocopy or on a separate piece of paper attached to the copy or photograph, noting when and where you saw or copied the item and where the item is now or who has it.

Write down other useful information about the items you find. For instance, if your aunt gives you a picture and says it is a picture of Great Aunt Sally taken when she was sixteen and living in Iowa—make a note not only of what your aunt told you, but also that she is the one who provided the information. To avoid confusion, use full names when referring to relatives. You know who Great Aunt Sally was, but record her name as Sarah "Sally" Martin Smith so others will understand, too.

Your note in the above example might be written as follows:

Photograph acquired 28 December 1989, from Aunt Jane Martin, 111 Main Street, Smithville, MD 22222. Aunt Jane said she had owned this picture for twenty years and it was given to her when her mother, Lizzie Martin Jones, died. She said that it was a picture of my Great Aunt Sarah "Sally" Martin Smith (sister to my grandmother Lizzie Martin Jones), who was well known to her, and was taken when Sally was about 16 and lived in Iowa.

It is important from the very beginning of your research to know who told you what, when they told you, and where each piece of information came from. Richard Lackey's book *Cite Your Sources*, written especially for genealogists, explains how to document each source and gives examples. Elizabeth Shown Mills' new book, *Evidence! Citation and Analysis for the Family Historian*, should be required reading for every genealogist. To help you understand how to cite your sources, examples of typical source citations are shown throughout this book. A novice researcher should be concerned with getting all the vital pieces of information about a source—writing the citation in perfect form can come later.

Suppose in the example just given, you are told later by someone the picture is of Great Aunt Malinda Jones? At that point you will have to weigh the evidence and decide which person's information should be more accurate, and, if possible, get another opinion about the identity of the person in the photograph. The evaluation of the evidence can only be done when you have cited the source of each piece of information as you collected it.

Gathering Oral History

After you've gathered all the papers and photographs from your own home and family, begin to gather the oral history, stories and traditions of your family. You have probably listened to family stories all your life. Write down what you've heard and the sources of the stories. Record as many details as possible. Every detail is a piece of information that may become an important clue in solving the mystery of your family history.

Next, interview relatives and any other people who may know something about your family. The older people in the community, especially those who lived near your family, may know a great deal about your family.

Using a tape recorder is the best method to record an interview, if your subject is agreeable. Often the person you're interviewing will be very conscious of the recorder at first, but will usually forget all about it within a few minutes. Be familiar with your equipment and have extra tapes on hand, so you don't disrupt the interview by having to stop every few minutes to adjust the recorder.

Prepare for an interview by making notes in advance about the questions you want to ask and by being familiar with the family you're asking about. When the subject of your interview talks about Aunt Sally, you should know who she's talking about.

Take your time during the interview; don't badger your subject by asking question after question and barely listening to the answers. Be prepared for a leisurely chat. Don't be annoyed or impatient when the person you are interviewing wanders off onto another subject. At the proper time, you can gently move the conversation back to your subjects of interest.

Don't let the interview go on too long, especially if the person you're interviewing is elderly. When your subject gets tired or bored, you will begin to hear many more 'I don't remember' answers. The more enjoyable the interview is, the more relaxed and informative the person you're interviewing will be. He or she will also look forward to hearing from you again when you're ready for another interview.

As part of your interview, remember to ask about documents, pictures, or old papers relating to your family. If you have any of these items yourself, bring them along to share with the people you're interviewing. It may help to jog their memories.

Immediately after the interview, transcribe your notes while everything is fresh in your mind. This is also a good time to note things you didn't have time or forgot to ask, so you'll be prepared for a follow-up interview. If possible, schedule a second interview about two weeks after the first.

Make a reference note for your interview. An example of this citation might be:

"Oral interview with Jane Martin Smith," 27 December 1989, by Carolyn Earle Billingsley. Recording (and/or notes) owned by Carolyn Earle Billingsley, Alexander, Arkansas. Note: Jane Martin Smith is interviewer's mother's sister, and was 87 years old at the time of the interview, conducted at her residence, 111 Main Street, Smithville, MD 22222.

You might want to send a copy of your transcription to the person you interviewed and ask if there are corrections or additions. Reading the interview transcript may trigger additional memories.

An Oral History Primer by Gary L. Shumway and William G. Hartley, contains many helpful suggestions about tape recording personal and family histories.

Even though you cannot visit each person you'd like to interview, you can conduct interviews by telephone, using the same guidelines as indicated for an in-person interview. The only factors which differ are the expense involved for the call if it's long distance, and the legal restrictions concerning the tape-recording of telephone conversations without the consent of the other party. Call when long distance telephone rates are lowest if convenient for the person you're calling. If you have the equipment to record telephone conversations, ask the other person if you may tape the call.

You can also obtain the kind of information you would obtain in a personal interview by writing letters to people you think may know something about your family. Remember, most people do not easily sit down and write several pages in answer to letters. You may find it best, at least in letters to non-researchers, to limit the questions in your letter to a very few. If your effort is successful, you can write again and again, with a few more questions each time [see chapter 10]. Always include a self-addressed, stamped envelope.

The proper way to cite information acquired in a letter, such as one your receive from your Aunt Jane, is as follows:

Letter, Jane Martin Smith to Carolyn Earle Billingsley, 27 December 1989. Original letter in possession of Carolyn Earle Billingsley.

Tracking Down Previous Research

Ask the relatives you talk with or write to if anyone in the family has already done some work on the family history. If so, contact this person, or locate a copy of his or her material.

Perhaps your great uncle was interested in compiling a family history and interviewed some family members fifty years ago. Someone in the family may have saved his notes or the letters he received from other relatives. These will be extremely helpful in your research.

The proper way to cite letters your Great Uncle Cecil received from your Aunt Jane Smith, and which you borrowed from his son and photocopied, is as follows:

> *Letter, Jane Martin Smith to Cecil Earle, 3 January 1949. Original in possession of John Earle, 333 Mesa Avenue, Palo Alto, CA 94306. Photocopy of original in possession of Carolyn Earle Billingsley.*

Identify a letter by writer, receiver, date, current location of the original letter, and the form of the letter you actually used. If your cousin sent you a transcription of the letter instead of the letter itself, your citation would be to the transcription, not the letter:

> *Transcription of letter from Jane Martin Smith to Cecil Earle, 3 January 1949. Transcription by Cecil Earle, 333 Mesa Avenue, Palo Alto, CA 94306, who retains original letter. Copy of transcription in possession of Carolyn Earle Billingsley.*

Finding Information In Cemeteries

Visits to family cemeteries will give you a great deal of information. Ask in your interviews and letters where various family members are buried. As you visit each cemetery, examine each tombstone carefully. Old, weathered tombstones are notoriously difficult to read, and many times dates have been copied incorrectly as 1873, when it was actually 1878.

Copy information from each stone and look for other family members or associated families buried nearby. Draw diagrams of the cemetery plots and label the graves not only of your family members, but also of people buried in adjoining plots.

Photograph tombstones of interest to you. Get down to the level of the stone and get a close-up shot. If the stone is not too badly weathered and the light is good, you should be able to read the information in the developed photograph. Write the name and location of the cemetery on the back of the photograph (or on a piece of paper attached to the back of the photograph), and the date you took the picture.

If you're visiting an out-of-the-way cemetery, don't rely on your camera alone to record information—always make a written record while you're there. If your roll of film was lost or damaged before you received your photos, you would still have your written notes. Save the last frames of the roll film and photograph a copy of your notes so you'll have a written record to store with your negative file.

Record the name and location of each cemetery in your notes and add pertinent notes to your diagram, such as 'There are three unmarked graves in the Smith lot.' The proper way to cite an inscription from a tombstone for your Grandmother Thomas is as follows:

> *Headstone inscription for Susan Thomas, Pleasant Grove Cemetery, Saline County, Arkansas (1 mile north of Highway 5 on Midland Road). Photograph taken 27 December 1989, by Carolyn Earle Billingsley.*

If the cemetery is a large one and still in use, you can probably locate the sexton or caretaker and inquire about records. Cemetery or burial association records may show the names of people buried in unmarked graves or list the name and address of the person who paid for the plot. Even a rural cemetery may have a groundskeeper who can direct you to the person in the neighborhood who knows details about who is buried in the cemetery.

Take care when visiting abandoned cemeteries. Never cross private property without permission and never go unaccompanied to remote or dangerous areas. You may want to check with the appropriate state agency about the dates for hunting seasons before you venture into backwoods areas.

For further information on researching, recording and preserving cemeteries and tombstones, contact The Association For Gravestone Studies, 30 Elm Street, Worcester, MA 01609.

3 - Organizing Your Family Records

A Filing System

Now that you have gathered all these papers, notes, and photographs, you need to organize them in some way so you can find what you need without digging through stacks of papers. However, your system shouldn't be so complicated you spend more time filing than doing research.

Devise a system of your own or use another system that works well for you. If you think you want to use a formal, prepackaged system, investigate *Managing a Genealogical Project* by William Dollarhide. Computers can help you organize your information, but you'll still want a paper system of group sheets and family folders.

Any system of organization is better than no system at all!

Genealogists will tell you, as disorganized mountains of paper grow, they wish they had adopted a system from the beginning and stuck with it.

The system described below works well. If you are just beginning your research, use this system from the start. After you have been researching for a while, you may want to modify this system or change to another. Even if you change to another system, all the work you have already done will be readily accessible if your data is organized in this manner.

Supplies you will need to organize:

- File cabinet or boxes to store files in
- Paper or printed forms to record data
- Black ink pens
- File folders
- Looseleaf notebook (not spiral)
- Index dividers for the notebook

Many companies offer printed forms for sale and you will probably eventually prefer to use them.

Use black ink—you will be making many photocopies of your records as you research your family history and it is important for your work to photocopy well.

Family Group Sheets

Make a record about each nuclear family. Use a sheet of paper or a pre-printed family group sheet form. Write the names of the parents of each family at the top with the husband's name first. (If you try to be liberated and write the wife's name at the top, you will be thoroughly confused before long!)

After the husband's name, leave some space, then write the wife's name. (If you are using a family group sheet form, it will be much easier, since you will simply fill in the blanks.)

Use full names, and always use the maiden names of women. If you don't know a woman's maiden name, just write her first and middle names and leave a blank space to be filled in later. Some families require more than one sheet of paper for all the information you will be recording.

Make a separate family group sheet for each marriage. If a man was married five times, he will have five family group sheets; one for each marriage.

Start with yourself and your spouse, or your parents if you are not married. Work backward in time, generation by generation, putting the names of each married couple at the top of a page.

Beside each name write the date and place of birth, marriage, death and burial. Genealogists customarily write all dates with the day as a number, the month spelled out and the year in four digits: 5 August 1948. Leave blank space where the information is not yet known.

List each of the couple's children in birth order down the left margin of the page, recording the date and place of birth, marriage, death and burial for each, as well as full name of spouse.

As you record each piece of data, write the source of your information and any additional information you want to note, such as religion, occupation, or military service, on the back of the paper or family group sheet form. You may have conflicting information from two or more sources; the family Bible may have one date for your grandmother's

FAMILY GROUP SHEET

Husband's Code ....
Wife's Code ....

HUSBAND'S NAME _John Smith_
Date of Birth _2 FEB 1902_ (2) Place _____
Date of Death _11 MAR 1970_ (1) Place _NEWPORT, JACKSON CO., AR_ (1)
Present Address (or) Place of Burial _WALNUT GROVE CEM., JACKSON CO., AR_
His Father _JAMES SMITH_ (2) His Mother's Maiden Name _SARAH JONES_ (6)
Date of Marriage of HUSBAND and WIFE on this sheet _2 JAN 1923_ (3) Place _LAWRENCE CO., AR_ (3)
Check here if there was another marriage: By husband ☐ By Wife ☐ Was this couple divorced? Yes ☐ No ☒ When?_____

WIFE'S MAIDEN NAME _MARY EARLE_ (Use separate sheet for each marriage)
Date of Birth _5 AUG 1904_ (7) Place _JACKSONPORT, JACKSON CO., AR_ (7)
Date of Death _____ Place _____
Present Address (or) Place of Burial _512 ELM, NEWPORT, AR 72112_
Her Father _ABNER EARLE_ (7) Her Mother's Maiden Name _AMY DAVIS_ (7)

Items of interest about the above couple (occupations, hobbies, achievements; social, civil, and political activities; physical descriptions—include photos if possible; military service; cause of death):
JOHN SMITH: CARPENTER, MASON, MEMBER SHADY GROVE METHODIST CHURCH, NEWPORT, AR; CAUSE OF DEATH: HEART ATTACK
MARY EARLE SMITH: ELEMENTARY SCHOOL TEACHER 1930-1962 NEWPORT, AR

Use reverse side for additional information

Have family sheet	CHILDREN (Arrange in order of birth)	Code	Birth Information	Death Information	Marriage Information
1	AMY LOU	(4)	on _7 FEB 1924_ (4) at _LAWRENCE CO. AR_ (3)	on ____ at ____	on _(NEVER MARRIED)_ to ____
Y 2	JOHN EARLE	(4)	on _8 MAR 1926_ (4) at _JACKSON CO. AR_ (4)	on ____ at ____	on _10 APR 1947_ (8) to _BETTY ADAMS_ (8)
3	ABNER	(4)	on _9 APR 1928_ (4) at _JACKSON CO. AR_ (4)	on _12 MAR 1929_ (5) at _JACKSON CO. AR_ (5)	on ____ to ____
4			on ____ at ____	on ____ at ____	on ____ to ____
5			on ____ at ____	on ____ at ____	on ____ to ____

Check here if there are additional children ☐

Footnoting. To substantiate the information recorded on this page, please use the footnotes listed below. One of these numbers should be placed in the circle provided next to each answer on the questionnaire. If you got the information from a source not listed, place that source on a vacant line and use the number next to which it has been placed as your footnote number.

Use ① only if you have filled in the blank from personal knowledge (such as the name of your brother). If you must look up his marriage date, give as the source wherever you looked it up. If you asked him, give his name as the source.

① Name and address of person filling in this sheet. Date _12 MAY 1984_
SARAH SMITH, 123 MAIN ST., LITTLE ROCK AR 72201
② _UNION PENSION APPLICATION OF JAMES SMITH FILED 6 APR 1909_
③ _MARRIAGE RECORD BOOK P, PAGE 313, LAWRENCE CO., AR_
④ _BIRTH CERTIFICATES, AR VITAL RECORDS, SEE COPIES IN FILE_
⑤ _TOMBSTONE, WALNUT GROVE CEM., JACKSON CO. AR, SEE PHOTO IN FILE_
⑥ _MARRIAGE RECORD, BOOK F, PAGE 207, LAWRENCE CO. AR_
⑦ _BIBLE RECORD OF ABNER & AMY EARLE - SEE PHOTOCOPY IN FILE_
⑧ _MARRIAGE RECORD BOOK FE, PAGE 102, PHELPS CO. MO_

This family group sheet is for an imaginary family, but yours should contain the same elements, especially careful source documentation.

As you learn more about the family group, you will add more information and additional source notes. Copies of the documents you've referenced as sources will be filed in the folder for this family. This form, designed by Netti Schreiner-Yantis and used with her permission, is available from National Genealogical Society.

date of birth and her tombstone may have another. Record both dates on your family group sheet, with a note indicating the source for each date.

One of the best pre-printed family group sheets available was created by Netti Schreiner-Yantis. It is available by mail order from National Genealogical Society. On this form, at the end of each data entry space, there is a small circle in which to record a footnote number. A separate area on the form contains space for source citations. With permission from Netti Schreiner-Yantis, a sample of this copyrighted family group sheet form is reproduced in this chapter. Dallas Genealogical Society also sells an excellent group sheet with space for specific source citations.

If you very carefully note all of the sources you have used about a family, you will create a bibliography, that is, a list of sources, there on the group sheet. You won't have to carry copies of birth certificates, marriage records, census photocopies, and other original records, because you'll have a precise record of them on your group sheets.

Use index tabs to divide your looseleaf notebook into sections, with a separate section for each surname (last name). To start, label one section with your father's last name, one with your mother's maiden name, one for your father's mother's maiden name, and one for your mother's mother's maiden name. As you progress in your research, you will add more index tabs with new surnames you have found.

As you begin filling out each family group sheet (whether it's your own piece of paper or a pre-printed form) file it in the appropriate section of your looseleaf notebook by the surname of the husband. Put the most recent generation first and the oldest generation last.

Family Folders

Create a file folder for each family group. Use the last name first on the label. File each piece of documentation, or a copy of it, in the appropriate folder for the family to which it relates. For instance, place your birth certificate in the folder labeled with your name and your spouse's name; put your mother's baptism record in the folder labeled with your mother and father's name.

As you create each file folder and label it, file it in your file cabinet or box in alphabetical order by last name and then by first name. As with the family group sheets, there should be a separate folder for each marriage; hence, you may have five folders for one man—each folder relating to a different marriage.

You may find it helpful to keep a piece of paper in the front of each family's file folder listing the documents in the folder. It will serve as a sort of 'table of contents.' You may even want to cross-reference each document with a number, which will also appear on the 'table of contents' page. As your file folders grow larger and larger, this will save a great deal of time and keep you from shuffling through a file folder looking for a certain document you *think* you have.

You may also want to make copies of your family group sheets and put a copy in the front of each family's file folder for easy reference. When you receive a letter from another researcher working on your family and he asks you to "send everything you have," on a certain family, you can photocopy your family group sheet that lists everything you have instead of sending copies of dozens of records.

Pedigree Charts

A pedigree chart is a diagram showing your family lines at a glance and a sample is reproduced in this book.

When your pedigree chart is completed, lines will lead from your name back through the generations of your ancestors. Your paternal (father's) side of the family will be on the top half of the chart and your maternal (mother's) side will be on the bottom half of the chart. There will no doubt be many blank spaces when you begin and even after years of research there may be blank spaces. Don't be discouraged by these: each blank space represents a mystery and you are the private investigator seeking to solve that mystery.

Pedigree charts usually cover from three to nine generations, depending on how large the paper is on which they are drawn; but they can cover as few or as many generations as you wish. When a family line chart is filled in all the way to the right margin, that family line is continued on another pedigree chart.

Make your own or use pre-printed pedigree sheets because they are the 'road maps' that quickly show your family lines. Put copies in the very front of your loose-leaf notebook as a guide to your ancestors as you research.

When you are researching in libraries, archives, and courthouses, you will need only your notebook, as all the data you have gathered will be recorded on the family group sheets. You can note the places where you lack a piece of information and will quickly see what you need to look for in your research. You can also see the type of evidence or

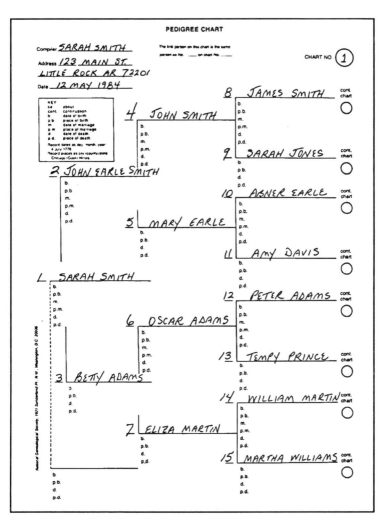

PEDIGREE CHART

Compiler SARAH SMITH
Address 123 MAIN ST.
LITTLE ROCK AR 72201
Date 12 MAY 1984

CHART NO. ①

The first person on this chart is the same person as No. _____ on chart No. _____

KEY
ca   about
cont.   continuation
b   date of birth
p.b.   place of birth
m.   date of marriage
p.m.   place of marriage
d.   date of death
p.d.   place of death
Record dates as day, month, year
4 July 1776
Record places as city (county) state
Chicago (Cook) Illinois

8 JAMES SMITH — cont. chart ○
4 JOHN SMITH
9 SARAH JONES — cont. chart ○
2 JOHN EARLE SMITH
10 ABNER EARLE — cont. chart ○
5 MARY EARLE
11 AMY DAVIS — cont. chart ○
1 SARAH SMITH
12 PETER ADAMS — cont. chart ○
6 OSCAR ADAMS
13 TEMPY PRINCE — cont. chart ○
3 BETTY ADAMS
14 WILLIAM MARTIN — cont. chart ○
7 ELIZA MARTIN
15 MARTHA WILLIAMS — cont. chart ○

National Genealogical Society, 1921 Sunderland Pl. N.W., Washington, D.C. 20006

This pedigree chart has been simplified to illustrate the order in which people are placed. On your chart, list places and dates of births, marriages, and deaths under each name. The upper half of the chart contains your paternal (father's) line, the lower half, your maternal (mother's) line.

documentation supporting each event if you have carefully cited your sources.

Be certain the notebook you take with you has your name, address and telephone number in a prominent place on the front cover in the event you inadvertently leave it behind. Keep copies of all your charts and forms in the family folders you leave at home, so if your notebook is lost, you can recreate it.

Research Notes

As you research, record notes or information about only one family (or surname) on each sheet of paper. For instance, if you are going to the library to seek information on your mother's Martin family and your father's Smith family, do not make notes on both families on the same sheet of paper. It not only becomes confusing, but think about it, where are you going to file your notes if they cover several families?

At first, it may seem as if this practice wastes a lot of paper, especially if you record just one small bit of information on your Martin family on a full sheet of paper, but you will find it saves you a great deal of confusion in the long run.

After each interview or visit to a cemetery or library, take your notes from the day's activities and 'post' the new (or different) information on your family group sheets and pedigree charts, recording the source for each piece of data on your family group sheets.

File each document you have photocopied and each photograph you have developed and all notes you've taken in the appropriate file folder. If you have a lot of photographs, you may want to invest in a good photograph album. In this album, use index tabs, labeled with your various surnames, in the same manner you have used them in your loose-leaf notebook, and file the pictures accordingly.

Some people prefer to recopy or retype their notes, but it is not necessary. Keep in mind, each time data is recopied, errors multiply, so you may wish to stick with your original notes.

Correspondence File

Another file that will be helpful to you is a correspondence file. Use file folders for this purpose. Each time you write a letter to anyone concerning your family research, file a copy of the letter in your correspondence file, in the back of the folder [see chapter 10].

Keep copies of all letters you write. If you are using a computer, print out an extra copy of each letter; if you have easy access to a copy machine, make an extra copy of each letter before you mail it; if you use a typewriter, use copy sets, carbon paper, or pre-printed correspondence forms that come with a duplicate page; if you write your letters by hand, either use carbon paper or photocopy each letter before you mail it.

When you receive an answer to a letter, pull your copy of the original letter from the file (it should have worked its way to the front of the folder), attach it to the reply, and file both in the appropriate family file folder.

The oldest letters will work their way to the front and the most recent letters will be in the back. You can see at a glance if a letter was written months ago and you have received no reply, you need to follow up on it.

You may wish to keep a record or correspondence log of the letters you send. Remember, when writing for information, enclose a self-addressed, stamped envelope. [see chapter 10 for more information].

Archival Filing Supplies

Ordinary paper is manufactured with acid and becomes brittle and yellow over time. You can buy archivally safe paper, file folders, and photograph albums to safeguard your records. The materials are more expensive, but if you're concerned about the long-term storage of your records, you may want to make the investment. Much of the paper manufactured today has an alkaline base and is much more permanent than the acid processed paper sold just a few years ago.

Certain types of plastics and adhesives used in photograph albums are especially dangerous. There are many suppliers of archival materials, one of which is Light Impressions, PO Box 940, Rochester, NY 14603. Call 800/828-6216 for a free catalog. Creative Memories, a company with many local sales representatives, sells a variety of albums for long-term storage of family memorabilia. Call 800/468-9335 to ask for the address of a Creative Memories representative in your area.

As you spend time and money collecting genealogical information about your relatives, think about protecting your collection from disasters. You may want to contact a microfilming company about filming your records. (Look under "Business Services" in your telephone directory.) You can record over 3,000 images on one roll of microfilm and store it in a safety deposit box at your bank. Mark the pieces of paper that have been filmed so in a year or two, you can go through your records and make another roll of film with the new information you've added.

You might want to photocopy your family group sheets from time to time and exchange them with a researcher working on the same family. In case of a fire, flood, or tornado, your records could be reconstructed. Don't wait until a disaster happens, make plans now to protect your records and photographs.

Photography

If photography is your hobby and you can use a 35mm, single-lens, reflex camera, you can copy old photographs, documents, and Bible records with your camera. A good source of information about this is *Photographing Your Heritage*.

Use your camera and/or video camera to make a permanent record of tombstones, living relatives, family reunions, heirlooms, and historic structures. When using your camera, make a list of what you have photographed as you work. Consider photographing the list with the last frame on the roll of film. Introduce the people you are video-taping at the beginning of each segment, also noting the date and place.

Store copies of your negatives separately from your photos. Consider exchanging negatives with a friend or relative in case a fire or natural disaster destroys your original photos. Store negatives in archivally-safe sleeves and notebooks and include a list with each set of negatives listing who, what, when, and where.

Photographs and documents can be scanned, or converted into computer image files, with the proper computer equipment. Copies of the computer files can be stored and easily shared with other researchers.

Using Libraries and Archives - 4

Primary and Secondary Sources

Now that you've set up a record keeping system and assessed your home and family sources, it's time to explore libraries and archives. Libraries are where you will look first for published records and manuscript collections. Archives are where retired official records of public or private agencies are kept. In some cases archival facilities may contain many of the same types of materials as libraries. Both have two broad categories of records available to you—primary and secondary records, or original and compiled sources.

- Primary records are those created at or about the time an event occurred. They are often referred to as original records. When conflicting information arises in your research, primary sources are more apt to be correct than secondary records.

- Secondary records, sometimes called compiled sources, were created at a later time than the event. For example, marriage records entered in the appropriate volume of county records by ministers and justices of the peace shortly after the marriages were performed are primary records. An index to those records created many years later is a secondary source. Secondary sources can be very helpful in locating primary records, but remember to always attempt to locate and use the primary records. Remember too, that because a record is not listed in an index does not mean that record is not among the original records.

Records vary widely in their accuracy. A death certificate, for example, is probably an accurate source for the date and cause of death because the record was made about the time the event occurred. However, it may be very inaccurate regarding the deceased's parents' names and the deceased's place of birth because these events occurred long before this record was made.

You must learn to evaluate sources in terms of how accurate they may be. Not everything you see in secondary or even in primary sources about your family will be true. It's up to you to learn to be a good detective. Noel C. Stevenson's *Genealogical Evidence: A Guide to the*

Standard of Proof Relating to Pedigrees, Ancestry, Heirship and Family History, and Elizabeth Shown Mills' *Evidence! Citation and Analysis for the Family Historian* are very helpful guides.

Libraries

Compiled or secondary sources can be very helpful in leading you to primary records. Published family histories, compilations of census records and tombstone inscriptions, local history publications, and other books may contain information about your family.

How do you find these books? Visit your local library and look at the genealogy collection. Sometimes local or community libraries are on a limited budget and cannot afford the expensive reference works you need and you will have to visit a larger, regional library. Most larger libraries have a collection of local history and genealogical materials for their area, but many also have collections that include books and reference materials about surrounding areas.

If you do not live near a library in an area where your family resided for many years and you need information about libraries in another state, your local library may have a directory of libraries which will give you the address of the library in the area for which you need materials. *The Handy Book* lists libraries, archives and their addresses. You may also ask at your local library about inter-library loan although most genealogical materials do not circulate.

Each state has a state archives and state library, and although their collections generally center around their own state, they often include a broad collection, especially of secondary sources. For example, the Arkansas History Commission in Little Rock has not only materials about Arkansas, its collection includes a vast array of materials about the American South and the states surrounding Arkansas. Some state archives are more complete than others. Investigate yours.

Finding Aids in Libraries

Larger libraries often have *Genealogies in the Library of Congress: A Bibliography* by Marion J. Kaminkow. This reference series and updates to it list genealogies in the Library of Congress in Washington, DC, and tell you how to get copies of the books from the Library of Congress if you cannot locate them locally.

Netti Schreiner-Yantis published four editions of *Genealogical and Local History Books in Print*, a catalog of genealogical and local history books which may lead you to helpful information. Genealogical Publishing Company in Baltimore is publishing the fifth edition of the series, edited by Marian Hoffman. More than a bibliography, this series tells you not only what books have been published, but where to buy them.

Ask your reference librarian for additional finding aids to books about genealogy and local history.

Many family histories have been written in the form of articles published in genealogical and historical journals. These have been indexed in various forms. Donald Lines Jacobus began an indexing project of genealogical periodicals which was carried on by Inez Waldenmaier and is now being done by Laird C. Towle. Annual volumes are published as *Genealogical Periodical Annual Index.*

The Genealogy Department of the Allen County Public Library has compiled a massive index to thousands of articles in genealogical periodicals. *PERiodical Source Index,* edited by Michael B. Clegg and Curt B. Witcher, indexes articles by locality, family surname, and research methodology. Many libraries have this set. Read the introductory remarks in a volume of *PERsi* to learn about how to use the set and how to search for articles mentioned in it.

Source Citation: A Reminder

When you find published materials about your family, read them very carefully, looking for references to primary source materials such as wills, deeds, probate records, and Bible records. Just because the information is in print doesn't make it true. When you take notes from published materials, be sure to record enough information about the book or article in which you found information so that you could pick up your notes ten years in the future and find the book or article again. Photocopying the title page is a quick, easy way to create a citation. You can note the copyright information usually found on the reverse of the title page and the name of the repository right on that photocopy.

When you use a book or search a record and *don't* find any relevant information in it, make a source record anyway and note what you looked for and that it was a negative search.

Complete source citation is especially helpful when inconsistencies in your research arise and you must evaluate your findings. If you exchange research data with others working on your family lines, other researchers will respect and appreciate thorough source citation.

If you decide to write your family's history, you will need all your source notes. Richard Lackey has written a helpful guide about citing sources in genealogical materials. For more detail than Lackey provides, read Elizabeth Shown Mills' *Evidence! Citation and Analysis for the Family Historian*. Generally, record the author, complete title, publishing company, date of publication, and the name of the library where you found the book. A typical family history book citation would be:

> Buchanan, Jane Gray, *Thomas Thompson and Ann Finney of Colonial Pennsylvania and North Carolina: Lawrence, Closs and John Thompson, Allied Lines of Finney, McAllister, Buchanan, and Hart (Oak Ridge, Tennessee: Privately Published, 1987). Copy in private collection of Desmond Walls Allen.*

Genealogy and family history books are often produced in very small publication runs, sometimes less than five hundred copies. For that reason, they frequently cost more than mass-produced books printed by large, established publishing houses. Because of the small press runs, they become increasingly difficult to locate as time passes. Standard scholarly footnote and bibliographic forms do not list the repository, library, or archive where a book is found, but it is a wise precaution with potentially rare books. Pay special attention and note revised editions or books to which addenda have been appended.

The Family History Library

The largest genealogical library in the world is the Family History Library in Salt Lake City, Utah. The Church of Jesus Christ of Latter-day Saints is collecting copies of both compiled and primary reference materials from all over the world and making them available to researchers through a network of Family History Centers. Write to the Family History Library or call a local LDS Church to learn the location of a Family History Center near you. Volunteers in these centers welcome researchers of all faiths.

If you are thinking of making a trip to the Family History Library in Salt Lake City, J. Carlyle Parker has written a practical guide for beginning researchers. Jim and Paula Warren have written *Making the most of Your Research Trip to Salt Lake City*, based on their many years of leading groups of researchers to the Family History Library. Consider going on a planned group excursion to Salt Lake City.

Other Collections and Associations

There are many nationally-known libraries with genealogical collections. National, regional, and local genealogical and historical societies often have libraries and publish material useful to researchers. To locate those groups, consult the following sources. Mary K. Meyer is the compiler of *Meyer's Directory of Genealogical Societies in the USA and Canada*. The Federation of Genealogical Societies publishes a membership directory with detailed information about its member societies.

The Genealogical Helper, the most widely-known genealogy magazine, publishes a list of societies by locality each year in the May/June issue.

The March/April issue of *The Genealogical Helper* lists family associations and their publications which may be helpful to you. A family association is a group of researchers working on a specific surname or descendants of a particular ancestor. The purposes of these organizations are to share research information, spread news of reunions, keep cousins updated about living relatives, and other efforts toward unity. Through a local society or family association, you may find much of your research has been completed by distant family members. Larger libraries should have copies of Meyer's directory, the FGS directory, and back issues of *The Genealogical Helper*.

Searches in Primary Sources

Many libraries have copies of primary source material in addition to the secondary sources mentioned above. When you have thoroughly searched your home and family sources and set up a record keeping system, you are ready to search for printed material about your family. When you have found (or failed to find) helpful printed material about the family and location of your interest, it is time to begin research in primary materials.

Newspapers

Libraries and archives have a variety of research materials available to you and sometimes it is difficult to decide where to begin. Look at your group sheets. What information are you missing? You are looking for names, dates, places, relationships and any other information about your family that will help complete a meaningful portrait of them.

One important primary source is newspapers. Your search through home and family sources probably turned up some brittle, yellow clippings—probably obituaries. The clippings are fragile because newsprint paper was designed as a cheap way to spread today's news and it wasn't and isn't made to endure. Fortunately, many newspaper collections have been microfilmed and are available at archives and libraries.

Old newspapers have marriage, birth and death notices, 'personal' or gossip columns, legal notices, announcements, advertisements and more. Reading old newspapers published in a time and place your ancestors lived can be very time-consuming, but also rewarding, not only for details about your family, but as an overall record of the times.

Church newspapers can be very useful if your ancestor was an active member of a group that published regularly.

Manuscript Collections

Libraries and archives have a variety of unpublished papers in their collections that can be very useful to genealogists, but it seems like a huge task to even an experienced researcher to locate materials in manuscript collections. You must consider what records were created that might mention your ancestors, then you have to find the records.

Diaries, journals, collections of letters, church records, plantation accounts, and store ledgers are examples of the types of manuscript records that might exist. These records are unpublished, meaning you cannot find copies as you would locate copies of books.

Consider a sample case: Perhaps the country doctor who delivered your ancestor's babies and attended your family's illnesses kept a journal of his visits. Your family probably had no idea he wrote down the date, time and cause of your ancestor's death. When the doctor died, perhaps his papers were packed in a trunk and stored away. When his widow died, the house was sold and one of the married granddaughters kept the doctor's old trunk. Perhaps she and her family moved to Oregon, and some descendant of hers kept the old trunk but donated the papers to a medical school library, thinking they would be of some use there. Now you need the information but have no idea the papers even exist.

The National Union Catalog of Manuscript Collections, a multi-volume series made up of entries submitted by custodians of manuscript collections, can guide you to the right collection. This series is arranged by subject and location and is updated regularly. A surname index to part of this series, *Index to Personal Names in the National Union*

Catalog of Manuscript Collections, 1959-1984, has been published by Chadwyck-Healy, Inc. of Alexandria, Virginia. There are other finding aids to manuscript collections, but this is the most well-known and the largest. The best way to learn about it is to contact a reference librarian in a university library near you and ask her to show you the set and explain how to access the information in it.

Libraries and archives are increasingly making information known about their collections by offering access through the Internet [see chapter 13] to their catalogs.

Knowing the names of families associated with your family can be especially helpful in finding and using manuscript collections. Who was your family's minister? Who was the captain of your ancestor's militia unit? Who was the justice of the peace in your family's neighborhood? These are the people most likely to have left collections of personal papers behind. As a beginner, you are probably not ready to dive into manuscript collections, but you can be alert for the names of people and activities that might have created written records.

Pitfalls of Spelling and Handwriting

Before you begin research in primary records, a caution should be issued about spelling and handwriting.

You will find, in old records, spelling was informal and inconsistent. Do not dismiss the name 'Hewes' if you are searching for 'Hughes.' In an early census enumeration, census takers reportedly spelled the surname 'Reynolds' thirty-four different ways. As you get deeper into genealogical research, you will become an expert at guessing how many ways a name may be spelled (or misspelled).

Another factor related to spelling is the common use of nicknames in old records. Since families often repeated the use of first names among fathers, sons, grandsons, uncles, nephews, and among mothers, daughters, aunts, grandmothers, and cousins, people were sometimes known by nicknames.

Consider the following substitutions: Polly for Mary, Patsy for Martha, Betsy or Lizzie for Elizabeth, Shabby for Bathsheba, Fate or Mark for Lafayette, Felty for Valentine, Sally for Sarah, and many others.

Naming patterns have changed throughout past centuries. Our founding fathers had, for the majority, only two names, a first or given name and a surname: Benjamin Franklin, George Washington, Thomas

Jefferson. A trend developed for middle names and sometimes even three given names were possible for an individual.

Many American families in the newly created United States named sons for prominent heroes and political figures: George Washington, Thomas Jefferson, Benjamin Franklin, Francis Marion, Marquis de Lafayette, Andrew Jackson, Martin Van Buren, William Henry Harrison, James Monroe, James Knox Polk, and others. This practice leads to finding an 'O. H. P. Jackson' in census records—named for Oliver Hazzard Perry; or a 'J. K. P. Smith'—named for James Knox Polk.

When succeeding generations began naming sons for this generation, you find Wash Jones named for his uncle, George Washington Jones; or Fate Smith, named for his uncle, Marquis Lafayette Smith; or Jack Davis, named for his uncle, Andrew Jackson Davis. Frank James of the famous James Gang was probably named for some male relative named after Francis Marion, the Swamp Fox.

After the War Between the States, names such as Robert E. Lee Bearden, Ulysses S. Grant Davis, Jefferson Davis Cates, Stonewall Jackson Smith, and Patrick Cleburne Jones began to appear.

The study of naming patterns is a detailed subject in itself, and, as a beginner, be alert for naming patterns in your family and the possibility of nicknames being overlooked in a search.

A man's name may have changed over time. James Robert Smith may have been called Robby as a child to distinguish him from his father James. If you are searching for Mr. Smith in the census records, hoping to find him as a child in his parents' household and do not investigate a name change, you may miss the record you are seeking.

Be creative in imagining variations in names. A prominent researcher was temporarily stumped in a search for Marcus Aurelius Davis. No luck on the problem in searching beyond the obvious for Mark, M. A., A. M., or Ary. How was he listed? Why, Reelus Davis, of course.

Some relationship words we use today did not have the same meaning in times past. Junior and Senior which today usually refer to a father and son, were used in the past to mean younger and older. Cousin was a loose term indicating some relationship, but not necessarily the precise relationship we know today. Brother and sister may have meant fellow religious group members. Write down the relationship terms you find in the records, but do not ascribe modern meanings to them until you are certain from other sources of the significance of the words.

Reading old handwriting is a learned skill. Books have been published to help you recognize unusual letter forms. Especially helpful is E. Kay

Kirkham's *How to Read the Handwriting and Records of Early America*.

- One of the most unusual letter forms you will encounter is an old style double s, written as a 'ps' or an 'fs' to the untrained eye. Names like Moss and Ross turn into Moff and Roff; or Jeffe for Jesse.
- Capital letters S and L, T and F, I and J are difficult at times to tell apart.

As a beginner, while you are searching handwritten primary records, ask for assistance or make a photocopy for later aid in deciphering handwriting. To make a better guess at an unknown capital letter, compare it in the same document to a word you recognize beginning with the same formation. If you cannot distinguish Samuel from Lemuel, compare it elsewhere in the record written by the same person to 'State' or 'Statute' or 'Signed,' words you know begin with an S.

Your Personal Frame of Reference

Remember, primary records are those created on or about the time of the occurrence of an event. You must use your own frame of reference about the day-to-day business of life and come to understand the types of primary records your ancestors were creating.

- You probably remember a visit from a census taker, the counting of the United States population that takes place every ten years. Census takers also visited your ancestors.
- You may have filed deed and mortgage papers at your local county courthouse for your real estate. Your ancestors did, too.
- You pay real estate and personal taxes at the county level and your ancestors did, too.

In order to find the primary records you need for your research, you must have an idea about how the records were created, where they were created, how they are filed, and where copies of the old records are stored now.

The next chapter of this book deals with federal census records, one of the most helpful primary sources to genealogists.

5 - Federal Census Records

Census records are one of the most valuable primary sources created by the federal government. Large groups of census enumerators counted the United States' population every ten years beginning in 1790, because our government is based on equitable representation in our legislative branch. As with all primary sources, you must know how the records were created, where they were created, how they are filed, and where copies of the old records are stored now.

For detailed information about the directions given census enumerators for each census, *Twenty Censuses: Population and Housing Questions, 1790-1980* explains all the questions asked in a particular census year. In general however, enumerators visited each family in their districts and asked a set of specific questions. Those questions and the format in which they are recorded varied throughout our history, moving from just a tally by age, sex and race of how many people lived in a household, to much more detailed information in recent times.

A comparison of the information found in the 1800 federal census and the 1900 federal census will illustrate not only what you can expect to find, but the dramatic increase in information available in more recent years.

Since reapportionment, the original purpose of the census, was based on geographic location, the census was compiled according to state and county. That is how the records are filed. To locate past census records about your family, you must know or find the family's geographic location in a census year.

Finding Census Records

The 1920 census is the most recent available to researchers. The 1930 census is due for release for research by the general public in 2002. With your ancestors in mind, from information from older relatives and family knowledge you have collected, you must create a picture of the probable family groups and where they lived in 1920. For example, if you know your grandfather was born in 1911, and you know the names of his brothers and sisters and his parents and have a general idea of the area in which the family lived, you can probably locate the family in the 1920 census with your grandfather listed as a nine-year-old child.

However, you must have access to copies of the census records. The National Archives in Washington, DC publishes copies of census records on rolls of microfilm. (Microfilm is a long strip of photographic material containing reduced images of printed material. You must use microfilm on a specially designed microfilm reader or viewer which enlarges the images.) The National Archives publishes catalogs of its holdings on different subjects, census records being one of the most popular. The National Archives has copies of census microfilm for all available places and years. Regional branches of the National Archives also have large selections of census microfilm.

Libraries and archives with genealogical collections have census microfilm for selected places and years, mainly those of primary interest to their patrons. Libraries and archives generally have a brochure describing their collections, including census microfilm. You can locate archives and libraries with significant genealogical and historical holdings in a directory published by the Association for State and Local History, available in most libraries.

When you have the addresses, write to libraries and archives in your areas of interest and request brochures describing their major holdings. Ask each institution about its policy of answering questions by mail. Some require special forms. A general rule is to ask one specific question about one person in your letter and wait for a reply. Don't forget your SASE (self-addressed, stamped envelope). Some facilities charge an additional fee to answer out-of-state requests.

If you cannot locate a library or archive facility within driving distance, you may borrow census microfilm through Church of Jesus Christ of Latter-day Saints (LDS) Family History Centers mentioned in the previous chapter. AGLL, a large vendor of genealogical materials, rents census microfilm for use in your home. If you do not have a microfilm reader, you may rent the film from AGLL and use it at your local library as almost every library has a microfilm reader available for public use. You may also contact your local library about their participation in microfilm rental and interlibrary loan programs.

Using Finding Aids

People listed in census records are in enumeration order, grouped by county and state. By the twentieth century, and earlier in some areas, there were so many people to list, unless you know a very specific location for the family you are researching, you will need a census finding aid. These take the form of Soundex indexes published on microfilm for 1880, 1900, 1910 and 1920.

Soundex indexes to federal census records were made by the Works Progress Administration (WPA) during the 1930s. The Social Security program had been recently introduced and the government saw the need for large numbers of people to prove their ages when they became eligible for assistance. These finding aids were created on a statewide basis and grouped like-sounding surnames by a numerical code. There were restrictions on which families from the census records were included. Libraries and archives which have the microfilm rolls of this finding aid have directions for computing the codes and more specific information about the criteria used for including families. These indexes are published by the National Archives and are listed in their census catalogs.

Many private companies and individuals have indexed census records and published these indexes in book form and in electronic format on CD-ROM. Some are statewide, others by individual county. Some are very accurate and complete, others are filled with errors and omissions. To a genealogist, using census indexes to best advantage comes with experience and practice. Use the indexes, being very creative about spelling possibilities, but do not rely on them entirely. Just because a person isn't listed in an index doesn't mean he wasn't in the original record. If you do not find the family you are seeking in an index, look for those allied and associated families you have been recording as you do your research, and go directly to the census film and search the county where you think they should have been.

Using Census Records

The best method for using census records is to start with the most recent available to you and work backward in time, relying on clues found in the census to guide you. Remember not to skip a census year because you *think* you know what you'll find in the record. An elderly relative may have been enumerated with the family in the year you skipped, giving you a new name and new set of clues for your search.

Unfortunately, census records are prone to a variety of errors. The census enumerator did not tell us from whom he obtained the information he recorded. Perhaps a neighbor supplied the names and ages of the family members. Using your personal frame of reference, imagine what answers your neighbors would give about your present family to a census enumerator. Even if the enumerator received correct information, he may have written it incorrectly. He was working from the spoken word, translating it to paper. The copyist may have made errors. Accept what you find in the census records with a grain of salt, but record the information just as you find it—make no effort to 'correct' the record. And cite your source!

A typical citation might be:

> *1850 United States Census (Free Schedule), Wayne County, Tennessee; page 200, family 304, dwelling 302, lines 12-18; National Archives Microfilm M408, Roll 315.*

Census records for 1920, 1910, 1900 and 1880 list more detailed information about families than earlier census records. For these years, relationships between family members are stated. Sometimes a person in a household is listed as a 'boarder', but watch for clues in other records, because the 'boarder' may actually be a relative. The reported birthplaces of the parents of those enumerated are listed by state or country.

The census records for 1870, 1860 and 1850 list the names of everyone in the household and other valuable information, but relationships among the people in a family are not stated. You must be careful to prove relationships with other records.

For example: You may find an 1850 federal census record listing William Smith, age 30; Sarah Smith, age 27; and three little Smiths, ages 8 and under. To eliminate the possibility of Sarah being William's unmarried sister living in his household, caring for her widowed brother's children, you must examine other records.

Or, for example, a man and woman are listed in the 1870 census with a string of children, stair-stepped in age: John Jones 48, Mary 47, Sarah 18, Emily 16, Albert 14, Jesse 12, Mary 10, and Margaret 8. Are these all the children of the couple, or are Mary and/or Margaret grandchildren? Suppose an older son was killed in the War Between the States, his widow remarried, and left their minor children with the paternal grandparents? Without further investigation, you can't assume what the relationships are.

Records kept at the county level, including marriage, deed and probate records, can be helpful in establishing relationships of people found in census records. In the previous example, a guardianship record for Mary and Margaret may show them as daughters of Samuel Jones, deceased. The 1860 census for the Jones family might show Samuel, his wife, and infant daughter Mary. A marriage record for the county might reveal who Samuel's wife was. A dower relinquishment might

Comparison of Census Information
a Century Apart

1900

- Location: State, county, township, street, house number
- Full names of every household member
- Relationships of each person to the head of household
- Race, Sex, Age
- Month and Year of Birth
- Marital status, Years Married
- For women: mother of how many children and how many living children
- Person's birthplace (usually the state)
- Father's birthplace
- Mother's birthplace
- Year of immigration to US
- How many years in the US
- Naturalized?
- Occupation
- Able to read, write, speak English?
- Attended school how many months?
- Home or farm - ownership or rental
- Date enumerator visited each family
- Additional remarks

1800

- Location: State, county, town or division
- Names of heads of family only
- Numbers of Free Whites
    Males&Females under 10
    Males&Females 10 - 16
    Males&Females 16 - 26
    Males&Females 45 & up
- All other free persons except Indians
- Slaves
- Date the census was turned in

establish that Mary was the wife of John. The 1850 census might show Samuel in the John Jones household. [see chapter 6 on courthouse research]

On your family group sheet for John Jones, you would post the information about the family you pieced together from the records and carefully cite all the sources you used.

Census records of 1840 and before list only the name of the head of the household with tally marks by age, race and sex of the other people in the household. You have no way to know if the people represented by tally marks have the same last name as the head of household or are even related.

Remember county and state boundaries changed over time and since that is how census records are filed, you must be aware of these changing political boundaries. Your ancestor may have lived in one place but changing political boundaries can cause him to appear in census records for different counties in different years. *The Handy Book* published by Everton Publishers lists county formation dates, years for which federal census reports are available, and the names of parent counties. William Thorndale and William Dollarhide's *Map Guide to the US Federal Censuses, 1790-1920,* is a wonderful resource showing the evolution of county boundaries.

Why no mention of the 1890 federal census? All but a small fragment burned in 1921. Some early census reports are missing as well for other areas.

While the most popular census records are the federal population schedules, there are other census schedules for researchers to comb for information. Other schedules or parts of the federal census list different information.

- Mortality schedules, available for 1850 through 1880, list people who died during the twelve month period preceding the census enumeration. Many of these schedules have been abstracted and published. Norman E. Wright's *Preserving Your American Heritage*, lists the location of these schedules.

- Slave schedules, available for 1850 and 1860, list slaves by age, sex and color under the owner's names.

- Agricultural schedules, 1850 through 1880, list farmers' names, crop information, and acreage.

- Manufacturing or Industry schedules list the names of people who had businesses and include statistics about the activity. They were taken as early as 1810, although most for 1810 have not survived.

Records for 1820 have been compiled and published by the National Archives in microfilm form. Schedules for 1850 through 1880 exist in various records repositories.

- Revolutionary War pensioners were specially noted in the 1840 census. The 1890 census listed a special schedule of veterans and their widows. Unfortunately, the veterans' schedules only exist for Kentucky and the states through the rest of the alphabet. The states' schedules listed alphabetically before Kentucky were destroyed in 1921 with the 1890 population schedules. Many of the existing veterans' schedules have been published in book form and on CD-ROM and all are found in National Archives publication M123, on microfilm.

In addition to the federal government, states or territories often conducted census enumerations. A list of these has been published in *State Census Records* by Ann S. Lainhart.

Remember the Neighbors

For all the census years, one of the most valuable categories of information, sometimes overlooked by beginning researchers, is neighbors of the family of your interest. Census information was taken from house to house, neighbor to neighbor, down the streets and roads. When you begin census research, look carefully at other families in the census records after you discover your family. Families with the same surname as the one you are researching will be of particular interest, but look also for similarity of unusual first names and coincidental places of birth. Families seldom moved alone from one area to another; they moved in groups related by blood, marriage, religion, ethnic origins, and social cliques. Tracking groups of people across the country through time in the census records can be easier than tracking a single family.

In the example given previously in this chapter, researching the John Jones family can be especially challenging. But if you find Samuel married the daughter of Bartley Abernathy and other in-laws of the Jones' included the Huddlestons, Bledsoes, and Rutherfords, you'll have more names to look for in previous places of residence. People tended to marry within their own social and economic groups—identify groups of people to look for in census records.

When you abstract a census record on your family, don't just copy the record for one family. Write down complete abstracts of several families who lived nearest yours according to the microfilmed records.

Note the last names of the families within several pages of yours in the records. Study the birthplaces listed and if it appears your family moved from one state to another, look for other families in the neighborhood whose family members have similar birthplace patterns.

Federal census enumeration occurred only once every ten years. You must fill in the other years with primary material from other sources. You want to find the records your ancestors created while doing their day-to-day business and most of those are found in county or other local jurisdictions. That is the subject of the next chapter.

6 - Courthouse Research

The records in county court houses and other local jurisdictions contain information about your ancestors' day-to-day business. Deeds, wills, mortgages, marriages, probate records, court records, taxes and more were recorded in county records. The key to getting the most from county records is knowing where your family lived so you can discover where they went to transact their business. Remember political boundaries changed over time. Consult *The Handy Book* for county formation information or use William Thorndale and William Dollarhide's *Map Guide for the US Federal Censuses, 1790-1920* for maps of county evolution.

Learning About Your Family in County Records

- Marriage records contain women's maiden names, in addition to the marriage date. Sometimes parents' names, the ages and residences of the couple, and possibly the place the marriage took place are recorded. There are other helpful clues in marriage records, such as the religion of the minister performing the ceremony.

- Deed records show not only purchases and sales of land and other property, they often show divisions of estates among heirs. Tracing the land your ancestors owned can lead you to important clues about origins and relationships.

- Sometimes a person left a will, a document that directed how his estate should be divided at his death. More often, people died intestate, that is, without leaving a will, and the laws of the probate court determined how his personal property and land would be sold or divided. In both cases, there should be a probate court file in the country records unless the person was very poor or the family settled the estate informally among themselves.

- Studying tax records over the period of time your ancestor lived in an area can reveal a variety of information.

- Civil and criminal lawsuits are filled with interesting material.

- In addition, there are many other miscellaneous records in court-houses that can be helpful to you. Marks and Brands books, county court records and others can yield intriguing information.

Before you plunge into courthouse records, take some time and study the local history of the area where your ancestors lived. Examine information you have gathered from all sources and recorded on family group sheets to see what additional information you might expect to find in county records. Know what facts you need in advance of your research. Write some research objectives, that is, what you need to know and where you hope to find the information.

County records are available in places besides the actual courthouse. The Church of Jesus Christ of Latter-day Saints (LDS) is undertaking a massive microfilming project of selected records from courthouses all over the United States. You may be able to borrow the film you need through the Family History Centers of the LDS Church. State and regional archives may have copies of the LDS microfilm of county records. In addition, archives repositories may have additional county records, not filmed by the LDS, on microfilm.

County records have been a popular indexing and transcription project for many individuals and groups. These compilations make the records more accessible but you must remember these are secondary sources and if you find something of interest, you should go to the original record, the primary source. As these materials are published, they are often advertised in genealogical magazines such as *The Genealogical Helper*.

Unfortunately, many county records do not exist because they have been destroyed by fire, flood, vermin, or neglect. *The Handy Book* by Everton Publishers lists general information about existing county records. Counties with significant record loss are referred to as 'burned counties' by genealogists. Burned counties are a setback to researchers, but do not always present an insurmountable problem. Alternate sources exist for 'burned counties', such as copies of tax records kept by state auditors, superior court appeal records, manuscript collections, private abstract companies, records of surrounding counties, and others. When you encounter county record loss crucial to your research, think of it as a learning experience, an opportunity to become a creative genealogist.

Your searches in county records will be aided by your understanding of both the court system and the land record survey system used in your area of interest. Court systems differ from state to state and from one time period to another.

A land survey system is the method used to divide land into identifiable parcels so it can be described in deed records. Two of the most common land survey systems are the rectangular survey system and the metes and bounds system. Paul W. Gates has written, *History of the Public Land Law Development,* a very detailed book about the development of the United States land system and his book should be available to you in your local library or through interlibrary loan. To learn about the rectangular system, read *Subdivisions of the Public Lands* by J.S. Higgins, a reprint of an 1894 textbook on the subject.

- Briefly, the rectangular system is used from the Midwest through the western states and involves a grid of numbered ranges and townships superimposed on the landscape. A typical land description might read, "SW 1/4, Section 10, Range 11 West, Township 4 North, of the Fifth Principal Meridian." Once the survey was established, the descriptions remained stable even though state and county boundaries changed.

- The metes and bounds system uses a verbal description of boundaries, referring to water courses, natural features, and man-made markers. A typical land description might read, "Beginning at a red oak upon Roanoke River at letter A, John Smith's corner, thence due North 344 poles to a pine (B), thence S83E 107 poles to a sweet gum..."

Both systems have advantages and disadvantages. There are other survey systems; these are the ones you might encounter first. Learning the system used in the area of your interest will help you understand the records you find. Land records can be found at county, state and federal levels. For a thorough discussion of land records, see Val D. Greenwood's *The Researcher's Guide to American Genealogy.*

Visiting a Courthouse

When you have exhausted sources for county records and published secondary sources about your county of interest, it's time to plan your visit to a courthouse. Going with a friend experienced in courthouse research is a wise idea, but even a beginner with prior study and a plan can do successful research in a courthouse.

Know what you want to know before you go. You may browse after you get there, but you should have a definite plan about the items you wish to find. If you need a copy of a very specific document, you may be able to write to the proper county official and obtain what you need. Chapter 10 on queries and correspondence has more information about this topic.

When you decide to visit a courthouse, call or write in advance and inquire about business hours, holidays, renovations and other activities that might close the records to you. Call again just prior to leaving if your trip will be lengthy—you do not want to arrive and find a black wreath on the clerk's door that says the office is closed for the staff to attend the funeral of some prominent county official who died two days before your visit. Election day, just before and just after, is a poor time to visit.

Jim and Paula Warren have written a very helpful book, *Getting the Most Mileage from Genealogical Research Trips.* Follow their advice to maximize your travel success.

In the courthouse, most records are in large, bound volumes kept through the years by officials charged by law to maintain them. The old books contain handwritten copies of the papers filed in the clerk's office. The signatures in the books are not the signatures appearing on the original documents; they are copies made by the clerk. After the original documents were copied into the books, they were returned to the appropriate person, or filed in packets at the courthouse. Documents relating to a civil or criminal court case, probate court case, or chancery (if the state had chancery courts) case were usually folded and filed in paper jackets called packets. Those packets contain the 'meat' of the information; only a summary appears in the large books. Ask where and how the case file packets or 'loose papers' are filed.

Most of the record books have some sort of index. Study the indexing system but do not rely entirely upon it. The record you need may be indexed under a name you are unfamiliar with. Knowing the names of the people associated with your family, the people who migrated to the area with your family, appear near them in census records, and married into your family, will help you find 'hidden' information in county records about your family. These people acted as witnesses to legal documents, served as administrators of estates and guardians of minor children, and bought and sold land with your ancestors.

When you arrive at the courthouse and find the office that houses the records you require, remember you are probably not a taxpayer in that jurisdiction and you are interested in records not often used by the clerk's staff. Our wonderful democratic system allows us to elect a brand new courthouse crew periodically and while the records may still be there, the people who filed them usually are not. Records that are not used on a day-to-day basis may be filed in an inconvenient place, possibly unknown to the present staff.

Often the office personnel will be very friendly and delighted to have an out-of-town or out-of-state visitor. The clerk's staff may be even more receptive to your needs, *if* you observe a few of the following do's:

- Do dress in a reasonably dignified manner (no party animal t-shirts or swim suits, please).
- Do leave small children elsewhere.
- Do speak briefly about your research objectives (no lengthy family stories).
- Do use courtesy, and complain about nothing.
- Do expect photocopies to be expensive.
- Do your homework and know some basic information about the land survey system and court system used in the area so you will understand the answers to your questions.
- Do remember to express your thanks for assistance so the next genealogist to visit might receive a warm reception.

Take thorough notes and remember to make source citations. A typical citation for material you find in a courthouse might be as follows:

> *Will of Thomas Keesee, February, 1872, Ashley County, Arkansas, Will Book A, page 63. Office of the County Clerk, Hamburg, Arkansas. Certified copy in possession of Carolyn Earle Billingsley.*

If you had searched the above records on microfilm in the state archives or LDS Family History Center, you would note in your citation might look like this:

> *Will of Thomas Keesee, February, 1872, Ashley County, Arkansas, Will Book A, page 63. Genealogical Society of Utah microfilm roll 923456.*

Even though the record is on microfilm, it is still a primary record. If, however, you took the information about the will from a published book, your citation to the secondary source might be:

> *Mary Smith, Ashley County, Arkansas, Wills, 1850-1888. El Dorado, Arkansas: Smith Publishing Company, 1989, page 6. Allen County Public Library, Fort Wayne, Indiana.*

When citing to courthouse records, write the precise title of the record, give significant dates, list the location of the record, and the form (original or microfilmed) you used.

Remember the Neighbors

A reminder again, while you are searching county records, be alert for the names of the neighbors and allied and associated families you have been recording for your family of interest. Notice who witnessed deeds and who performed marriages for your family. If you sift through county records for one individual, you may miss important clues found in records left by friends, relatives of a different surname, in-laws, church brethren, business associates, and others.

In the case of Thomas Keesee, you should make notes about the names of the men who witnessed his will, the executor, the people who appraised his property, the people who bought property at the estate sale (if there was one), the new owners of real estate formerly owned by the deceased, the guardian of any minor children, a possible new husband for the widow, and the people who submitted claims to the estate for money owed them at the time Thomas Keesee died.

Pointers to Other Records

County records are very useful in themselves, but when used in conjunction with other records, they help contribute to a meaningful picture of your ancestors. In the case of Thomas Keesee's will mentioned above, other records to be searched might include cemetery inscriptions, funeral home ledgers, newspaper obituary files both in the place of death and previous place of residence, church minutes, fraternal organization records, and the family Bible.

No set of records should be used in isolation. Always think creatively about what other records might have been created, then look for those records.

7 - Military Records

As you research your ancestors back through time, consider their participation in wars. Remember, you are searching for circumstances and events that created records with genealogical value. Military service often creates two kinds of records: service and benefits from having served.

The National Archives in Washington, DC, is the largest repository of military records in the United States. An entire microfilm catalog is devoted to military records. Copies of those microfilm publications have been distributed throughout the United States and are available at major libraries with genealogical collections.

A Starting Point

Read a basic United States history text to learn more about the wars in which our country has been involved. Our government began with a war, the American Revolution, 1776-1783. We fought Great Britain again in 1812 and lost many records in a fire in Washington DC, the nation's new capital. In the early 19th century, we fought a series of wars with various Indian tribes. In 1846-1848, we fought a war with Mexico over Texas' entry into the union. The bloodiest of all our wars was the War Between the States or Civil War, fought between 1861 and 1865. We participated in the Spanish-American War in 1898, a war for independence for Cuba and the Philippines. World War I, once called the Great War, involved the United States in 1917 and 1918. 'Modern' wars, World War II, Korea, and Vietnam, are within living memory of many Americans.

Wars through World War I involved two kinds of soldiers, regulars and volunteers. Regular soldiers were what we think of today as career service people. Volunteers were civilians called into military service to meet an emergency. Sometimes "volunteers" were drafted into service, but they were still considered volunteers. Most of the wars listed above were fought, for the most part, by volunteers. If your ancestor was a career soldier, his records will be filed in different groups of records than those of volunteers.

Following the pattern of working from known information to unknown, from present to past, begin by identifying your ancestors who would have been of an age to have served in one of the wars mentioned above. Look first in home and family sources for evidence or family tradition about military service.

Look for pension records. The federal government has given financial assistance to people who were disabled in military service and to the dependents of those killed in the line of duty. Papers associated with a veteran's pension, which represented an important source of income to the family, were often kept in a safe place. As you interview older family members, ask if your ancestors received any sort of government payment—it may have been a military pension.

Look for the headstone of an ancestor suspected of being a veteran. His military unit may be inscribed on it. Most War Between the States military markers are upright slabs, curved on the top for Union veterans and peaked for Confederates.

Do your census and county record research first. You will need to know names, ages, places of residence and wives' and widows' names for your ancestors who might have served in the military.

War Between the States Union Pensions

The War Between the States, 1861-1865, (referred to by a variety of names, including 'Civil War') involved a large percentage of American men in military service. Most of the men who fought in this war were between the ages of 18 and 35, although in the South, the age range was wider, from 16 to well over 50. If you have male ancestors born between 1826 and 1846, (1811 to 1850 in the South), look carefully at the records associated with those men for possible military service.

Looking for a pension record first is a research shortcut because it is sometimes difficult to positively identify a soldier from his military record as your particular ancestor. There is an index on microfilm, *General Index to Pension Files 1861-1934*, National Archives microcopy T288, to pension applications based on Union service between 1861 and 1916. Most are based on War Between the States service. The cards in this index are arranged alphabetically by the veteran's name and list military rank, unit, term of service, names of dependents, filing date, application number, certificate number and state from which the claim was filed.

If you are relatively certain your ancestor received a Union pension, you may submit a request for a copy of his pension record without consulting the index. Follow directions below about obtaining and submitting form NATF-80, but be very thorough in giving information requested on the form so you will receive the right record.

Larger libraries and archives have copies of the *Index to US Military Pensions* microfilm publication. If you find a possible ancestor in this source, order a copy of the pension file from the National Archives on form NATF-80. Write the National Archives and request several copies of this form as you must submit separate forms for pension, military and bounty land files. Follow directions on the form and be sure to write "Copy All Papers" in prominent letters on the form.

Union military pension files are often a rich genealogical source. Typically, a claimant had to prove and describe in detail his military service. Pages from Bible records, transcriptions of biographical statements, birth and marriage records, and a variety of documents are often found in pension records. Even if the pension application was not successful, the records are on file. Legislation changed the pension laws through time and many applicants applied several times, giving more and more details.

While pension claims sought by the veteran are rich, pension claims by widows can be gold mines, especially when more than one woman claimed a veteran's pension! These are called widow's pensions and contested widow's pension applications. When you request a veteran's pension file with form NATF-80, you are, in effect, asking for the widow's pension, too, if one was filed. When the file is located, the National Archives returns a copy of your form with a bill for photocopies. The current standard charge is $10.00 (1997) for 10 photocopies, but if you have written "Copy All Papers" on the form you submitted, the bill may be much higher. In this case, the higher the better, because you will receive more information.

War Between the States Confederate Pensions

The discussion so far has applied to Union military pension records. There were two sides to the War Between the States, and while the federal government was willing to provide pension benefits for Union soldiers, it did not extend those benefits to soldiers who served in the Army of the Confederate States of America. Those pensions, if any, were issued by the individual states of Alabama, Arkansas, Florida, Georgia, Kentucky, Louisiana, Mississippi, Missouri, North Carolina, Oklahoma, South Carolina, Tennessee, Texas, and Virginia. The important points to remember about Confederate pensions are:

- Confederate pensions were issued by the individual state governments of the states listed above.

- Eligibility was based on the state of residence at the time of the pension application.

- States' pension laws varied widely as to effective dates, qualifications, and benefits. These laws were changed through the years.

If you suspect your ancestor was a Confederate veteran and he was a resident of one of the above-mentioned states after the war, write to the state archives in that state for additional pension information. For detailed Confederate pension information, see *Where to Write for Confederate Pension Records* by Desmond Walls Allen.

Service Records for the War Between the States

If you are lucky enough to discover a pension record, your search for a service record will be simplified. From information in the pension papers, submit another form NATF-80 to the National Archives and request a copy of the service records. Again, write "Copy All Papers," on the form.

If you do not find a pension record, your search for a military record will involve additional research. You must know which military unit your ancestor served in to be reasonably confident in submitting form NATF-80 for his record. This is where your knowledge of where your ancestors lived when the war broke out and your careful collection of the names of allied and associated families will pay off.

Union and Confederate service records are in the National Archives. Some forty years after the war ended, a massive records management program created 'Compiled Service Records,' that is, most of the information about a particular soldier was extracted and filed in one package. There *is not* a master index to Union compiled service records. There *is* a master index for Confederate service records and there are state-by-state indexes for Union and Confederate military records.

Two excellent guides to federal archives materials have been published by the National Archives. They describe all the major record groups relating to Union and Confederate records. An additional helpful guide, *Confederate Research Sources: A Guide to Archive Collections*, by James C. Neagles, is available.

To locate your ancestor's military unit, study local histories for the area in which his family lived when the war started. The 1860 federal census should be very helpful. Look carefully at the family's neighbors in 1860. Study the men living in the area who were of prime soldier-material age (see previous note about birth years of War Between the States soldiers). Your ancestor probably did not ride off to war alone. He went with a group of friends and neighbors. Look at property values listed in the 1860 census records; the more affluent men typically served, at least initially, as officers.

When you have an idea what units were raised in the area your ancestor was from, and you know the names of the men he probably served with, you will have an idea of whether you have the correct service record when you find a man with the same name as your ancestor in military records.

Understandably, Union military records are more complete than Confederate records. Because you do not find a Confederate military record does not mean your ancestor did not serve. He may have served in a home guard unit never officially mustered into regular service. He may have served in an irregular unit not recognized by the Confederate Army. And, he may have served in the Union Army instead of the Confederate Army. Consider, too, many men in border areas served in both armies, often Confederate first, then Union as sentiment and military might changed their circumstances.

Service Records for Other Wars

Heavy emphasis is placed in this beginner's guide on War Between the States military service because (1) such a great percentage of men participated in that war, and (2) it is the most likely war in which a beginner will find an ancestor.

Records for World Wars I and II, Korea and Vietnam, are restricted under privacy laws. Contact the National Personnel Records Center, 9700 Page Boulevard, St. Louis, Missouri 63132, for additional information about service records for these wars.

World War I draft registrations are available from the Archives Branch, Federal Records Center, 1557 St. Joseph Avenue, East Point, Georgia 30044. Most males born between 1873 and 1900 were required to register and you may be able to find information on your ancestor even if he didn't actually enlist in the armed services. You must provide a complete name and even a street address if your ancestor lived in a metropolitan area. Some 24 million cards are on file and the current cost for a search and photocopy of any record found is $5.00.

Spanish-American War service records have been compiled and there are indexes for each state and special units. Many of these indexes have been published. There are compiled service records for the War of 1812, Indian Wars and Mexican War. Requests for these service records are made by submitting form NATF-80 to the National Archives.

Service records are of less help genealogically than records created when veterans applied for benefits because of their military service.

Other Benefits

When the American Revolution ended, the United States found itself short on hard money but blessed with nearly unlimited land resources. Small wonder the incentive plan for soldiers relied on grants of land. Grants of bounty land, land given by the government in recognition of military service, was standard procedure for military service through the Indian Wars, but was discontinued by the time of the War Between the States. No bounty land was given for War Between the States service.

When you are researching your ancestors' real estate, be alert for any mention of bounty land warrants. If you find such a reference, order, on form NATF-80, a copy of the veteran's claim file. Laws concerning bounty lands changed through the years. Two helpful books in understanding the process are James W. Oberly's *Sixty Million Acres: American Veterans and the Public Lands Before the Civil War* and Paul W. Gates' *History of the Public Land Law Development*.

The Homestead Act of 1862 required a five-year residency among other qualifications for obtaining free or cheap land. One provision of the law gave Union veterans credit toward the five years for the time they served in military service. Homestead patents are usually filed in county level deed records, and it is possible to pursue the homestead application back into federal records and sometimes discover a copy of a Union military discharge in the file.

Conclusion

Military research can be complicated by too many men of the same or similar names and too little information to distinguish between them. They key to solving this problem is thorough research in census and county records—get to know your ancestor.

Search for a pension record first in hopes of getting a free ride to the right military record. Find the cemetery marker or headstone for each ancestor suspected of military service—don't rely on a printed cemetery index that may not identify a stone as a military marker. That military headstone may have just the information you need. Be alert for clues in land records that indicate military service.

Study local history materials for the area where your ancestor lived when the war started to see what units formed there. Identify friends, neighbors, and associates in the census and county records and look for groups of men instead of just one man.

The United States is populated by people from all over the world, blended to form that special breed we know as Americans. You are probably the product of many nationalities and cultures intermingled in your genes. If your ancestors have not been in the United States for a long time, you may have closer ties to your ethnic origins than some Americans who need two hands and all their toes to count their Revolutionary War ancestors.

If you persist in your genealogical and family history research, your search will eventually lead to other countries, even if your ancestors came to the United States before the Revolutionary War. Many books and articles have been written about research in English, Irish, Scottish, French, and German sources. As a beginner, do not attempt to skip generations and target a possible immigrant ancestor based on similarity of name or family tradition. Prove each generation's links as you work backward from yourself to your ancestors.

As you become more knowledgeable about research methods and sources, moving from beginner to intermediate researcher, *The Source: A Guidebook of American Genealogy* may give you new insights into your investigation. Special sections are devoted to lists of sources about research in other countries' records. *The Source* has been updated and revised in a new 1997 printing.

While it isn't possible in the scope of this book to provide detailed information about examining all the research sources unique to special groups, the following list should furnish a starting place.

American Indians

Norman E. Wright's *Preserving Your American Heritage* has especially good coverage on the subject of Native American research. *How to Research American Indian Blood Lines: A Manual on Indian Genealogical Research* has interesting information and is especially thorough on Northwestern Indians.

While many families have an oral tradition of Native American heritage, it is very difficult, in most cases, to prove. When Indians were assimilated into white culture and no longer maintained a separate ethnic identity, they ceased to be officially recorded as Indians. The best method to trace Indian ancestry is to do thorough genealogical and family history research first, then begin to learn about the records available to document Indian lineage. Collateral relatives, especially those who did not lose their Indian identity, can be extremely helpful.

Black Research

Researching black American families is little different from standard genealogical research as far back as the War Between the States. Oral tradition is very important, even more so than for other cultures.

While most researchers think of blacks as slaves before the War, a significant number were 'free blacks' and their records are found in census and county records. For those who were slaves, plantation records, will and probate records, and deed records for white families associated with their families are informative. Slave schedules from federal census reports will be helpful in researching black ancestry.

The Freedmen's Bureau was created by Congress in 1865, to serve the needs of newly-freed slaves. Records of this agency are maintained by the National Archives and available in many state and regional archives and libraries. One microfilm catalog from the National Archives is devoted to black research sources. *The Black Family in Slavery and Freedom 1750-1925* by Herbert G. Gutman contains more information about black research.

Other Ethnic Groups

Special research aids have been written to help people find their Scandinavian, Polish, German, Hispanic, Irish, Scottish, Italian, Asian, and Eastern European ancestry. *The Source: A Guidebook of American Genealogy* has extensive bibliographies of helpful books and articles on genealogical research in foreign sources.

When you identify the country from which your ancestors came, go to your local library and borrow a basic history of that country. Read it with special attention to the time period your ancestor left. You'll learn about the social, political, and cultural forces that contributed to the migration.

When you follow your American ancestors back in time, you'll want to learn which ship they came over in. John Phillip Colletta's *They Came in Ships: A Guide to Finding Your Immigrant Ancestor's Arrival Record* is very helpful in understanding passenger arrival records.

The Church of Jesus Christ of Latter-day Saints (LDS) has microfilmed primary records throughout the world and these are available for use at the Family History Library in Salt Lake City and Family History Centers all over the United States. Everton's *Handy Book* has maps and lists of resources for many foreign countries.

9 - A Broad View of the Research Process

This book is presented in a step-by-step, linear form, chapter after chapter of what do to next, but research takes place in a circle. Yes, home and family sources come first, but the order in which you do research may be directed by what records are available to you or the information you can discover. As you do research in census records, you will find new counties to search for county records. As you find new information in county records, you will come back to census records to search for the new people you have discovered.

As you research, you will record information about births, marriages, deaths, and children on family group sheets. When you reach a standstill, you will analyze your problem, decide which records might help you, and try to locate those records. As you search records, you will go back to secondary sources as you discover new family names and new areas where your family lived.

Remember to cite your sources thoroughly as you work. Eventually, you will encounter conflicting information, and you must evaluate your sources and decide which is the best evidence before you can continue.

Allied and Associated Families

While you are looking for information about your family, use your own frame of reference. You are part of social, business, religious, and extended family groups. So were your ancestors. Look in both primary and secondary sources for groups of people. If you have a broad base of people to look for, you will not run out of information and hit a 'brick wall.'

Within your notebook of family group sheets, in each surname section, keep a sheet of paper headed 'Allied and Associated Families.' List the names of people you find in the records who are probably members of those social, religious, business, and related groups.

As you work through the research process, keep written, dated notes of your analysis, evaluation, and planning sessions. When you search a source without finding what you expected to find, you have learned

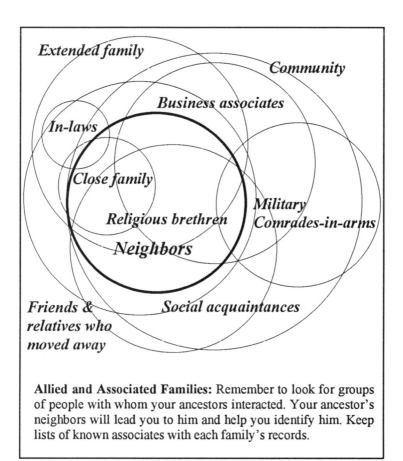

Extended family

Community

Business associates

In-laws

Close family

Military
Comrades-in-arms

Religious brethren

Neighbors

Friends &
relatives who
moved away

Social acquaintances

Allied and Associated Families: Remember to look for groups of people with whom your ancestors interacted. Your ancestor's neighbors will lead you to him and help you identify him. Keep lists of known associates with each family's records.

something. Negative research can be valuable. Record each search you make, even if you find nothing so you won't find yourself searching the same source twice for the same information.

Construct a 'research calendar' or 'log' showing the progression of your research. Write the title of each source you searched and whether the results were negative or positive. Beside each source, write the family names for which you conducted a search.

Same Name Problems

Your troubles are not over when you find the name of the person for whom you are searching in a record. Look in your telephone directory—how many William Smiths do you find, how many John Martins? You must not only find your ancestor, you must establish the record in question belongs to him, not to a man of the same name.

How do you do this? Look beyond the man's name to other identifying traits.

- If you ancestor is listed in census records as unable to read and write and, according to the census, has very little personal property and no real estate, he is probably not the man of the same name who wrote and signed a will, devising his many parcels of land and slaves.

- When you think you have found a marriage record for your ancestor, but you compute his age and find him to be about twelve years old, consider his father's younger brother or his cousin of the same name.

- Look for signatures of the man you've found as your possible ancestor. Compare them with signatures of the man you know is your ancestor.

- When you've found a man in the records with the same name as your ancestor, look at the names of the people around him. Who witnessed his deeds, for whom did he serve as administrator? Are these people on your list of previously established allied and associated families?

Study whole families, not single family units. Study families with your ancestor's surname who live in the same county or district. They may or may not be related. Learn enough about them to separate them from your ancestors. Perhaps the 'other' family in the county owned slaves and yours did not; perhaps they were Baptist and your family's members were Quakers.

Watch for markers left by previous record keepers who also had to distinguish between men of the same name. The tax records may have "of Wm." or "Sylamore" after a name to attach a father or place name to a man to distinguish him in the records from another of the same name. Believe that the man who owed the smaller amount of taxes made certain the clerk kept his records straight.

Maps

In the research process, maps are an indispensable resource. Libraries and archives have collections of maps and commercial firms sell reproductions of historical maps. Using census records without maps

---

is sort of like finding your way through your home blindfolded. You can do it, but you may encounter a few stumbling blocks along the way.

An especially helpful book, *Map Guide to the US Federal Censuses, 1790-1920,* has been produced by William Thorndale and William Dollarhide. It shows maps of the states through the years depicting changing county boundaries.

The Handy Book has current county outline maps for all the states, but there is a special feature about the maps—they show adjoining states and counties.

County maps come in various scales and are very useful for detailing plots of land belonging to an ancestor and his neighbors. Use Desmond Walls Allen's booklet, *Where to Write for County Maps* to learn the addresses of county map sources in the United States.

State lines may look like solid barriers on the map, but on the landscape, they're often invisible. Waterways on maps were barriers, but served as a means of travel as well. Look at topographic maps, maps showing natural contours of the land. Mountains were a real barrier to early travel. United States Geological Survey sells topographic maps in several scales. To order an index booklet and map catalog for the states you're interested in, call 1-800-USA-MAPS. Other government and commercial firms also sell USGS maps.

Look at soil maps. Your ancestors knew how to grow particular crops, and when they migrated to a new area, they looked for a region similar to their old home in terms of terrain, soil, and vegetation. If you find your ancestors in the Gulf Coastal Plain area of Arkansas, you can probably look a few generations earlier and find them in a similar region in Mississippi, Alabama, or Georgia. The agricultural schedules of the census will help you learn what crops your ancestors were raising.

Seeing the Big Picture

You must do two things well to be a successful genealogical researcher.

- Sift through volumes of records looking for minute details.
- See the 'big picture' or overview of your ancestors' lives in the context of part of an integral whole.

In other words, you have to be able to pan for gold dust, but take time to appreciate the clouds. Part of seeing the big picture is learning more about history.

Merely compiling names and dates is a very narrow view of family history research. Learning about political, social, economic, and religious events and movements taking place in your ancestors' lives can not only add 'meat' to the 'bare bones' of their vital statistics, it can increase your success in your research.

For example, reading about the "Great Awakening" (a religious revival movement in the early 1800s) can help explain why your ancestor became a Baptist or Methodist after a long family history of some other (or no) religion. Learning about the financial difficulties of cotton planters during the 'Panic of 1837' (a severe depression) can help you understand why your family pulled up stakes and moved westward at that time.

To get the full picture, frame your family within historical context. This is not to say you should sprinkle your family history with irrelevant facts. Avoid gratuitous information such as, "this was the same year Tyler was elected President" (unless your ancestor was active in the campaign or it had a significant impact on the family).

Frontier Press of Galveston specializes in books that can add important historical and sociological understanding to your research.

Reading for Historical Context

A lot of your library research time will be spent using genealogical sources you cannot check out. But you can visit the history section of the library and check out many books that will be helpful to your research, though they aren't traditional genealogical sources. We've already mentioned reading a history of the foreign country your ancestors came from. Read American history, too.

To structure your reading, begin with a broad overview of the social history of the United States. Read Daniel J. Boorstin's prize-winning trilogy, *The Americans: The Colonial Experience*, *The Americans: The National Experience*, and *The Americans: The Democratic Experience*. Earliest settlement through the founding of the United States is beautifully described in Ted Morgan's *Wilderness at Dawn: The Settling of the North American Continent*. His writing continues with *A Shovel of Stars: The Making of the American West 1800 to the Present*. Morgan tells the story with interesting people and vivid incidents.

Then narrow your reading, depending upon which time periods and geographic areas involved your ancestors. If your ancestors followed the most common migration pattern, they arrived on the American eastern seaboard and moved westward, seeking more land and greener pastures. Ray Allen Billington's *Westward Expansion: A History of the American Frontier* tells the details of this migration and includes a wonderful bibliography to direct you toward additional reading. If your ancestors chose in particular the southern route, read Everett Dick's *The Dixie Frontier: A Social History.*

David Hackett Fischer covers the cultural history of four waves of settlement from the British Isles in *Albion's Seed: Four British Folkways in America.* He tells about the Puritans who came to Massachusetts Bay, the Royalist elite and their indentured servants who came to Virginia, the Quakers who came to the Delaware Valley, and the Scotch-Irish who came to the American backcountry. Fischer tells of settlement and association patterns, religion, speech, architecture, ideas of family and marriage, child-naming patterns, customs of food and dress, and other aspects of every-day life.

Your reading will give you a better understanding of your ancestor's life, even if he isn't mentioned by name in a book. Researchers with ancestors who moved from Virginia to Kentucky can learn a tremendous amount about the forces which prompted the move and importance of the kinship networks by reading Boynton Merrill, Jr.'s *Jefferson's Nephews: A Frontier Tragedy.*

The books mentioned above are just a very small sample of the tremendous variety available. Frontier Press in Galveston carries many of these kinds of titles. Don't just look for books with your ancestors' names in them; look for books that can tell you about your ancestors' lives.

10 - Correspondence and Queries

One of the mainstays of genealogical research is correspondence. If you aren't adept at writing letters, it's time to practice. Today, telephone calls take the place of many letters, but unless you are especially wealthy or very impatient, letters must become a part of your routine. If you don't enjoy writing letters or have trouble thinking of something to say, you can turn that into a genealogical asset—your letters will be brief. Think of the person reading your letter when you write: how much does she need to know? Don't bore someone with meaningless trivia about your ancestors.

Two Categories of Letters

Letters generally fall into two categories: requests for information and sharing information with potential cousins.

Requests should be long enough to get your message across but short enough to waste no words. Be direct, be clear, and offer to pay for whatever you're requesting. Be sure you are writing to the proper person or agency.

Letters to potential cousins sharing your genealogical interest can be a bit wordier. Say who you are and why you want to know what you're asking. Don't overwhelm people with huge requests for all the information they have. Ask specific questions. You may want to leave space after each question so the recipient can just write in an answer. Better to be too brief in the beginning than have your letter laid aside because answering it seems like such a major literary event.

If you're writing a traditional letter on paper to send through the mail, you might include your photocopied pedigree chart, filled in with as much as you are certain of. If you are writing about a specific family, include a group sheet with your sources carefully noted.

Including a self-addressed, stamped envelope (SASE) for the convenience of the recipient of your letter is standard practice. Letters to federal agencies are an exception—your tax dollars should pay for the reply. Use a long, number ten, business size envelope with a one ounce, first class stamp affixed. Type, rubber stamp or print your name and address on the envelope in the area where the 'to' address goes and fold it in thirds to enclose with your letter.

Faxes and E-mail

Letters can take the form of faxed documents transmitted from one facsimile machine to another. The same rules apply to faxes that apply to letters in general, (except for the difficulty in sending a self-addressed stamped envelope via a fax machine). Do offer to pay postage on materials sent at your request, or to pay for the return fax call.

Many fax machines use thermal paper, an impermanent medium. Thermal paper isn't a concern in most business applications, because if not exposed to direct light, it will remain readable for a year or more. If, however, the information you receive on thermal paper has lasting value, photocopy it onto plain paper.

Faxes also come and go from computers, and are never actually printed on paper. Since magnetic media are also impermanent, print out the faxes you want to keep and file them with your permanent records.

More and more genealogical correspondence is taking the form of electronic mail messages (e-mail) sent via the Internet (more on this topic in chapter 13). E-mail is much more informally written than standard letters. Don't let this tempt you into failure to completely cite your sources in your messages. When another researcher e-mails you a request for information, consider the possibility that the message you're about to dash off may be forwarded around the globe to others interested in the topic. Be careful not to use obscure abbreviations or too many clever symbols specific to computer users—your message may not make sense when a printed copy is found in some manuscript collection in the next century.

Millions of e-mail messages shoot through cyberspace every hour. Most are successfully routed to their intended destination; some, however, never arrive. Ask your recipient to let you know your message was received. Acknowledge the messages you receive.

For information you receive via e-mail, cite to it just as you would a letter, and take the precaution of printing the message on paper to put in your files as you would a normal letter.

John Smith, john@seattlenet.com, "Abernathy Family."
14 February 1997. Personal e-mail to Ann Jones. Copy in
file.

E-mail addresses change even more quickly than residence addresses. To ensure your name and mailing address (not just your return e-mail address) appears on your e-mail messages, investigate the "signature" function of your e-mail program. A "signature" is several lines of text that will automatically appear at the end of each e-mail message you send, but you must first set up the text and turn the signature function on in your computer program. You can add your home mailing address, phone number, and even a short query, "Researching the Thompson family of Rowan County, North Carolina," to your signature.

Technical Tips

When sending traditional letters, add an enclosure line at the bottom of your letter listing the documents you are including. The abbreviation "Enc:" at the left margin below your signature is followed by notations, one to a line, of just what you are sending with your letter. This convenience serves three purposes: it gives the recipient of your letter a clear list of what to expect with the letter; it serves as a shopping list for you when you get ready to stuff the envelope; and it's a handy reminder to review when writing the same person again so you won't duplicate documents you've already sent. Your letters should always have your complete name and address and date on *every* page and *every* enclosure.

A fax cover sheet can serve to list the documents you're including in your faxed transmission. The cover sheet should list your complete name and address as the sender and the number of pages in the transmission. Fax machines are subject to all the mishaps of machinery, so include your phone number on the cover sheet so your recipient can call if all the pages you sent didn't arrive.

Enclosures, called "attachments," can be made to e-mail messages as well, in the form of computer files. Be sure the computer files you send as attachments contain your complete name and address. You can send family information pulled from your genealogy computer program as attachments to e-mail messages, or you can convert the information to text and include it in the body of an e-mail message. Consult your specific program manual for more information.

Dates in genealogy are always written with the day as a number, the month spelled out, and the year as a four digit number: 5 August 1948. An exception to this rule is made when you are transcribing a record—in that case, write the date just as it is written in the record. January wasn't always the first month of the year, so do not make changes in dates you find written in old records.

Use standard size, 8 1/2 by 11 inch paper. Smaller sheets get lost in filing and larger sheets must be folded before they are filed.

Make your correspondence the best quality output your machinery can produce. If you use a typewriter, use a fresh, black ribbon. Dot matrix computer printers are acceptable only if you use a quality ribbon and change it often. Paper should be the best grade you can afford. It needn't be expensive imprinted stationery; good quality white bond paper is affordable to everyone.

Genealogical correspondence has a way of staying around for a long time. For your handwritten materials, use black ink because it reproduces well. Always make copies of the letters you write. Even with a handwritten letter, you can slip a piece of carbon paper beneath your paper. With a computer or word processor, it is easy to produce two copies, one to mail, one for your files. Print out copies of your e-mail messages and replies that need a permanent place in your files.

Letters, copies of the letters you have written and answers you receive, should be filed with your other genealogical materials. See chapter 3, for more about filing correspondence. You may want to initiate a system of keeping track of which of your letters have been answered and which need follow-up correspondence. Val D. Greenwood's book, *The Researcher's Guide to American Genealogy,* suggests two systems for keeping a correspondence log. The simplest involves keeping a calendar listing four columns of information: the date of your letter, to whom and why it was sent, and the response.

Letters you write may surface in someone's files years from now. A query you place in a genealogical publication may lie hidden in a library for years until some researcher finds it. This makes address changes very important. Generally, the postal service will forward first class mail for one year if you file a change of address notice when you move. If you move frequently, consider adding a note about some 'permanent address' at the end of your letters. Give your parents' address or the address of some relative whom you believe will live in the same place for many years. Example:

> *PS: I am in military service and move frequently. Should future correspondence be returned to you, please write to me in care of Alpha Williams, 222 Oceanside, Baltimore, MD 22123.*

Electronic mail addresses change frequently. Fortunately there are Internet services which let you search for a person's e-mail address.

Queries

Queries are a specialized form of genealogical correspondence. A query is a brief request for information placed in a genealogical periodical, newspaper, or other means of communication. Most genealogical societies publish queries for members. Genealogical magazines such as *The Genealogical Helper* offer the opportunity to place inexpensive advertisements much like queries. Asking for information with a query implies your agreement to share your information.

To learn how to write a successful query, study those in genealogical publications. The best ones contain a reference to one family or individual and both the time period and place are mentioned. Lists of surnames being researched, especially if they are common names, are practically useless without additional identifying information.

Consider the following queries. Which would you be likely to answer if you saw a familiar name?

> *Researching Smith, Jones, Davis, Adams, Martin and Brown families of early North Carolina and Tennessee. Hopinfore A. Miracle, PO Box 123, Pittsburgh, PA 15901.*

Not very specific, is it? The following query is a better idea.

> *Seek parents of John Mitchell Lancaster born about 1809 in Smith County, Tennessee; died 1855, Izard County, Arkansas. Desmond Walls Allen, PO Box 303, Conway, AR 72033.*

Keep copies of the queries you submit just as you keep copies of all your correspondence so you will not have to recompose your queries when you submit them to another publication. If you're using a computer, save the queries in a file and just paste the blocks of text into your submission letters.

Follow exactly the query policy described in the publication you're submitting them to, both for content and method of submission.

The purpose of placing and answering queries is to coordinate your research activities with others researching the same family lines. Share and expect others to share. When you receive information from another researcher, you must evaluate it. Are primary sources of information cited? The material you receive from other researchers is a secondary source. It is often very helpful, but you must verify the work yourself. If you use information from another researcher on your family group sheets, be certain you cite your source as their material.

Family group sheet, "George W. and Lucy Birdsong Earle" compiled 20 August 1987, by Thelma Martin, 111 Main Street, Little Rock, AR 72002. Note: Mrs. Martin did not cite any sources for information contained on this family group sheet. Photocopy in possession of Carolyn Earle Billingsley.

Telephone Calls

Answers to letters you write to other researchers or responses to queries you have submitted may come in the form of telephone calls. Make a record of the date, caller's name, phone number, address and a summary of what you learned on a full size sheet of paper and file it with your correspondence just as though you had received a letter. Perhaps a cousin or fellow researcher mentions a burial site for a common ancestor and you want to add the data to your family group sheet. How do you cite a telephone conversation on a group sheet?

Telephone conversation with Roland Walls of Rolla, Missouri, 11 September 1985. Notes made at time of call in possession of Desmond Walls Allen.

You might also add a note evaluating the reliabilty of your informant's information and what her source is: personal knowledge, interview with relative, printed source, or something else.

Stop and think before you rush to the telephone to respond to a query. Many researchers object to being called early in the morning or late in the evening. Your call may come at an inopportune time. Write a letter and let the researcher answer at a convenient time with her files accessible. If you want a telephone response, say so in your letter, giving the best time to call and an invitation to call collect (that is, at your expense).

Electronic Queries

We'll say more about queries on the Internet in chapter 13, but remember all the things that apply to traditional queries also apply to inquiries in electronic format.

Submissions to specialized databases are also queries—they advertise your interest in a specific family. Everton's Roots Cellar and Broderbund's World Family Tree are two examples of this kind of database.

11 - Sharing Your Heritage

Involve Your Immediate Family

One of the rewards of genealogical and family history research is sharing what you have learned with other members of your family. You can involve your spouse and children in your research and make a true 'family affair' out of this experience. Imagine coming home from an exhausting day at the library and sharing what you have learned about your *spouse's* family—be sure to mention the part about 'horsethief' noted on the military service record and 'no account' written after the name in the tax records!

Involving your children in the research process can not only give them a sense of their heritage and ancestors, it can sharpen investigative and reasoning skills they can use in other areas of their lives. Many families today are scattered across the country and involving your children in family history can provide an opportunity for them to write letters to grandparents and cousins in distant places. Encourage your children to send electronic mail messages to grandparents who are computer users.

Let your family members specialize in areas of family history. If one member has an aptitude for computers, investigate a specialized program to manage family information (see chapter 13). Does a family member need keyboard practice for a class in school? There's your letter writer. Have the artist in your family illustrate your family history publication and design flyers about your family reunion. Post a map of the United States or the world and let the geography expert put map pins or sticker dots, color coded for different lines, on the map as your research progresses back toward the eastern seaboard and across the Atlantic.

Plan family vacations to ancestral areas. It is very rewarding to find cemeteries and home sites where your ancestors lived and visit the courthouses where they filed deeds and paid taxes.

Organize a Family Reunion

One way to share your information with family members and learn more at the same time is to organize a family reunion. Summer is the traditional time for families to choose a place to gather and visit. Reunions can be held as a one-time event, annually, or at other intervals.

How do you start? Call a meeting in person or by phone of the people in your family interested in getting together. Form a reunion committee. Pool your address books and make a list of all the relatives and cousins you know. Write a form letter, make photocopies of it, and mail them to everyone who might be interested in a reunion. Enclose a copy of your list and ask for more names and addresses. Appoint a List Manager.

Choose a date and place to meet. No date and place will suit everyone, but try to plan far enough in advance so vacation time can be reserved. When you decide on a place, be sure there are motel facilities available so family members won't descend on one household. If someone in your family has experience arranging meetings or seminars, let that person be Meeting Chairman.

Send reunion notices to everyone. Advertise the reunion in area newspapers, genealogical society publications, and genealogy magazines. Ask for a fee with registration or take up a collection at the reunion to defray expenses. Invite everyone to bring photo albums to display on a special table.

Plan special activities but leave unstructured time for visiting. Remember to have prizes for the oldest, the youngest, the person who traveled the longest distance to attend, the baldest, the couple married the longest time, the most newlywed couple, the tallest, and other categories. How about a contest to find the person at the reunion who looks most like a common ancestor? (Decision is by applause vote.)

Brainstorm with the reunion committee about creative activities to both entertain and tie the family together. Organize tours of family cemeteries in the reunion area. Make a wall-size display of a tree and let family members fill out and pin on paper leaves with their names and birthdates. Use waterproof markers and let family members draw their hand outline and sign a special tablecloth purchased for the occasion.

Be sure everyone at the reunion has a name tag printed with names large enough to be read in photographs. And take lots of photos! Record interviews on tape with older family members. Make a video tape with

---

a cameraman and 'reporter' who do mini-interviews with family members. Show videos of the last reunion.

Plan ahead for food and be sure the responsibility doesn't fall too heavily on too few people. Remember special dietary requirements for health and religious reasons.

Gather family information at the reunion. Remember to cite your sources as you write data on group sheets. Use the reunion opportunity to tell the family members what you have found in the records. You may want to compile the material you have gathered to share in a printed format.

Write Your Family's History

Whether for a reunion, an older family member's birthday, or no special reason, you may, at some point, want to write about what your research has uncovered. Don't wait to 'finish' your family history—there will always be one more generation or one more collateral line to research.

Choose a starting point. Perhaps you want to write about all the descendants of a particular ancestor, or you may want to write about a particular line of ancestors. You may want to just describe your research process and tell what you found in a logical, progressive fashion.

Before you begin to write your family history, read Patricia Law Hatcher's *Producing a Quality Family History.* Her well-written book describes methods, options, and information sources for producing a family history you'll be proud of.

Write what you know about your family, not what you imagine your family was like. Attempt to put your story in historical perspective, but avoid writing historical fiction. Above all, say how you know what you know. Let your ancestors speak for themselves through the records you have found. Don't jump to conclusions in your writing you cannot support with evidence. If you haven't investigated a record or can't solve a problem, say so—perhaps someone reading your book will take up the challenge. Depending on your audience, you can incorporate your sources into your narrative, or you can use footnotes.

You may want to include copies of group sheets and pedigree charts and copies of original documents and photos in your book. How much or how little you include is your decision. Above all, be sure your book has an index!

The Chicago Manual of Style will help you with the mechanics of assembling, formatting, indexing, and copyrighting your book.

You may want to print only a few copies of your book using a photocopier, or you may want to have a printer produce a few hundred copies using offset press. Your book may have paper covers or it can be hardbound. Your purpose and budget will help you make these decisions. Talk to folks who have published family histories; learn from their experiences. Read Pat Hatcher's book.

Writing about a portion of your family history can be a very effective way to analyze and organize your material. Missing facts, overlooked sources, new avenues of thought will occur to you as you write about your ancestors and your search for them.

If writing seems like an enormous task, there are resource materials to help you with style and grammar. William Zinsser's *On Writing Well: An Informal Guide to Writing Nonfiction*, and Sir Ernest Gowers' *The Complete Plain Words*, will help you.

Join a Genealogy Society

Another way to share your interest is to join a local genealogical society. It's a wonderful feeling to be among people who share a common passion. Ask your librarian if there is an active local society. Learn the name of a contact person and invite yourself to the next meeting.

Societies run on volunteer energy. Even if you don't have ties to the local community you can contribute your help to the society's projects. And perhaps someone else living in the area where your ancestors were from will be volunteering, too, even if she doesn't have local ties.

Inquire about state or regional genealogical societies. Ask about meetings and seminars. Often societies sponsor learning experiences for their members. Check *The Genealogical Helper Magazine* for a list of upcoming conferences around the nation. When you attend seminars and meetings, mix with the folks (this is called 'networking' in business circles) and share ancestors and research techniques.

Don't just read the publications of whatever society you join, get involved!

12 - Special Interests

As a beginner, there are topics which may be of only passing interest to you, but brief coverage here will give you at least working knowledge of where to go for more information.

Adoption

If you are adopted, you may want to know more about your birth parents. If you are not adopted, you may be interested in helping an adopted relative or friend discover information about her past.

In many ways, researching adoptions is different from the research you've been doing so far. You are now dealing almost exclusively with twentieth-century records. Since the people mentioned in these modern records may still be living, these records, such as hospital and Social Security records, are often confidential or harder to access, although some modern records, such as newspapers, telephone books and city directories, are easier to research.

One obstacle to the research of adoptees' origins is that the records or information was *deliberately* hidden. Your first step, therefore, is to gather all of the clues you possibly can—from relatives, neighbors or anyone else who may have known details about the circumstances of the birth. Use the interviewing and correspondence techniques discussed in previous chapters to contact these people.

Every adoptee's research problem is different and unique. Some have information about a parent's name or a birth location. Some have learned details about the circumstances of their birth or about siblings from conversations with relatives. You may have access to an original, unaltered birth record for the adoptee, or adoptive parents who want to help.

You must take what little you know and work from that point. If you know where the adoptee was born, put that together with the date of birth and consider ways to approach the problem. Was the original birth certificate altered? Did an announcement of the birth appear in the

Daily Record column of the local newspaper because the adoption didn't occur until the child was two years old?

If you know the name of the birth mother, search for all the families of that name listed in the phone book for that city in the year of the birth. Use a city directory for the year of birth to locate neighbors to interview. Use the cross-reference section to find who the neighbors were, then follow them up to the present in these same records.

Make a guess as to the age of the mother and research high school annuals. Locate some of the other students in the annual, and start asking questions about birth mother possibilities. Use marriage records to uncover the married name of women you're trying to locate.

Eliminate the word 'adoption' from your vocabulary when talking with public officials. In some cases, mentioning adoption can hamper your research efforts.

There are many groups working to help birth parents and adoptees get together. The International Soundex Reunion Registry, PO Box 2312, Carson City, NV 89702, allows people age 18 and over desiring reunion with next-of-kin by birth to file registration forms. Write for a form.

If you have a medical reason why it is important to locate your birth parents, find out about the laws in the state where the adoption took place. It may be easier to open adoption or hospital records for medical reasons.

Many adoptees and birth mothers are using resources on the Internet (see chapter 13) to locate each other. If you are a computer user and have access to the Internet, investigate the hundreds of information sites and news groups devoted to the topic of adoption.

Use your imagination, don't overlook a single clue, and be patient.

Twentieth-century Research

Twentieth-century sources can be very important for reasons besides adoption. Locating living cousins may turn up new information, Bible records, and photographs. A break in family continuity, perhaps caused by an early death or disappearance, can make using traditional genealogical sources difficult. It may be necessary to learn more about a father or grandfather who lived in relatively recent times before enough information emerges to move back into the nineteenth century.

Life in the twentieth century has been different than in previous times so different records have been created. The tremendous population increase due to birth and immigration, a shift from agrarian to industrial and service occupations, mobility offered by the widespread use of automobiles, and technological improvements in record-keeping ability influence family history research techniques. Conflicting legal trends—privacy vs. freedom of information—impact twentieth century research.

Creation of the Social Security Administration in the mid-1930's started a nation-wide accumulation of data about individuals. After the program began and current workers were issued account numbers, enrollment generally took place around the time a person entered the work force and requested assignment of a Social Security number. Initially, all workers were not included in the program, but gradually nearly all wage-earners came under the program. Now, because of federal income tax regulations, very young children are assigned numbers. The form to request a social security number, known as SS-5, contains information about an individual's parents' names and other potentially important clues for research. It is possible, under certain circumstances, to request a copy of form SS-5 filled out by another person. Form SSA-L997 available from Social Security's Office of Central Records Operations, Baltimore, MD 21201, has more information. Social Security Administration's Death Master File, a list of deceased persons who had social security accounts, is available through the LDS Family History Library system and through commercial vendors.

A wide variety of published directories contain helpful information to twentieth century researchers. Out-of-date copies of city directories and telephone directories are often available at larger libraries in an area of interest.

Using a personal frame of reference to imagine the variety of records created in recent times is essential; then research is a matter of finding the records, gaining access to them and interpreting the information found.

Compilations of all the telephone directory listings in the United States make people-finding easier. These databases are available on the Internet and for sale on CD-ROM in computer software stores. It's possible to search by name as well as by street address.

Immigration

Virtually everyone has ancestors who came to the United States from some other country. You may have one or more American Indian ancestors, but for the most part, some of your ancestors were immigrants.

The entire subject of immigration records is too complex to be covered in this book. The problems of a researcher working on an immigrant ancestor who arrived in 1910 from Italy are entirely different from a researcher working on an immigrant ancestor who arrived in Colonial times.

Remember, if your ancestor came to America from another part of the British Empire in Colonial times, he wasn't actually emigrating to a new country; he was simply moving from one part of his country to another, since what is now the United States was an English colony. What this means to you is that not many records were created in these cases, because not as much 'red tape' was involved.

You may know from which country your immigrant ancestor came, from your research in census or other records. The problem is determining *where* in that country the immigrant came from, so your research can continue. Knowing someone came from Germany is like knowing someone came from the United States: it's not very specific.

There are a variety of records that might lead you to the specific area of origin. One is immigration records. If your ancestor became a citizen, he had to file a Declaration of Intention to Become a Citizen. These were usually filed in the county where he resided. Later he filed a petition for citizenship or naturalization and these papers may also be filed at the county level. There was no standard place in county records to file these petitions, so you may find them in just about any kind of record book at the courthouse.

There wasn't much uniformity in how these applications for citizenship were handled in local jurisdictions. The first Naturalization Act was passed in 1790 and stated an alien who desired citizenship should apply to "any common law court of record, in any one of the states wherein he shall have resided for the term of one year at least." What this and later laws mean is these papers could be filed in just about any local, state or federal court. Twentieth-century laws required filing in federal courts.

Many families were very proud of an ancestor's citizenship papers and saved them. You may be able to find the originals. If and when you find the original papers or the court record of citizenship, these papers may tell you the specific area of origin, the date the immigrant arrived in the United States, and the immigrant's age. The form used after 1906 is very detailed.

The 1920, 1910 and 1900 census schedules recorded citizenship information for each individual, and these may be helpful to you in determining if your ancestor did indeed become a citizen, and what year he/she came to the United States.

Sometimes the census enumerator recorded the general area in a foreign country where the immigrant was born. Instead of merely writing 'Germany' for instance, he may have written 'Wurttemburg' (referring to the region, rather than the town). However, this is as if you knew your ancestor came from Oregon in the United States; it's more specific and very helpful, but you still need to know *where* in Wurttemburg.

There are other ways to determine the area of origin for your immigrant ancestor. Occasionally, when he died, there were heirs to his estate in the 'old' country, and the probate records might lead you to the area of origin. A biography in a book or an obituary from the newspaper may name a town of origin. The family Bible may tell where the family came from.

Old pictures of relatives who remained in the 'old' country may have been handed down in your family, and these photographs may have the name and town of the photographer who took them. Perhaps old letters from relatives who did not immigrate but kept in touch with the family who did will lead you to a specific area.

Many late nineteenth-century immigrants homesteaded land. This required them to prove citizenship and meet other requirements set by the United States government. The files for these homesteads can be ordered from the National Archives, and often yield important information—sometimes even a copy of the applicant's citizenship papers.

Passenger lists are one of the most useful records in determining the origins of immigrants. However, there is no centralized or complete list of these records. They are scattered, incomplete and difficult to use. You will find most of the existing passenger lists from about 1820 through 1902 at the National Archives. There are various indexes to some of these lists.

To search passenger lists, you will usually need to know the port of arrival, such as New York, New Orleans, etc., and the approximate date of arrival. If you also know the name of the ship, your search will be much easier.

When you have researched a branch of your family back to the immigrant ancestor and are ready to tackle these immigration and citizenship records and passenger lists, you should locate books at genealogy libraries that deal with these subjects in the time period and geographical area that apply to your case. John Phillip Colletta's *They Came in Ships: A Guide to Finding Your Immigrant Ancestor's Arrival Record* is a very helpful starting point in learning about this topic.

For more information on these records at the National Archives, you may want to read *Guide to Genealogical Research in the National Archives*. Another helpful source in understanding this subject is Greenwood's *The Researcher's Guide to American Genealogy*, which will lead you to other sources of information for immigrants.

Heirlooms

Your research in genealogy and family history may turn up family heirlooms and you may find you want to learn more about the items. Or you may find an object you think has historical significance and want to learn more about it.

Military arms and accouterments are very popular historical items. Bertram Hawthorne Groene has written a simple little handbook, *Tracing Your Civil War Ancestor*, to guide your research in this area. His book describes popular sources for more information about military artifacts.

Valuable jewelry pieces are often mentioned as bequests in wills or listed in inventories in probate records. Some states taxed gold watches and jewelry as separate items in tax records and you may be able to follow an item in tax records. Inscriptions on heirloom items of jewelry may have more meaning as your research progresses and you discover the names behind initials. Carefully examine old photos for unusual jewelry pieces—people often wore their "best" clothing and jewelry for a formal photographic portrait.

Publications about antiques can be helpful if you have an item and want to learn more about it. Your family heirloom may be an iron wash pot which family tradition says was brought from Virginia when the family moved westward. Look for mention of it in the inventories in probate records.

Quilts are a popular heirloom, often passed from one generation to another. Barbara Brackman's *Clues in the Calico: Identifying and Dating Quilts,* has a system of categorizing a quilt by fabric, style, color, technique and pattern to learn more about its origins. Quilts are sometimes mentioned in inventories of estates.

Historic Structures

Old houses and buildings have histories. They are designed, built, added to, sold, and resold. Interesting, even historic, events happen in them. Your interest may lie in the designer of a structure; the structure may be an old home place of one of your ancestors; or you may have acquired an old home and want to learn more about it.

The house may have an abstract of title that shows the history of the land upon which the house is built. Using the abstract or local deed records, work from known to unknown. Search for previous owners and neighbors who may have stories and photographs of the structure. Look for articles in local historical society periodicals about the structure. Look for the structure's address in cross reference sections of old city directories to locate previous owners, residents and neighbors.

Changes in the tax rates or assessment records will indicate when improvements were made on the land. Sanborn Fire Insurance Company maps are available for many areas and they show improvements and changes in structures on the land. These are often available at archives and large libraries on microfilm.

To learn more, contact National Trust for Historic Preservation, 1785 Massachusetts Avenue NW, Washington DC 20036. Ask for the address of your state's preservation office. *House Histories: A Guide to Tracing the Genealogy of Your Home* by Sally Light, and *A Field Guide to American Houses* by Virginia and Lee McAlester are very helpful sources.

Professional Genealogical Services

You may find it necessary or expedient to hire a professional to help with your research, either occasionally or full-time. There are alternatives to hiring a professional: you may find a distant cousin living in another state who can search local records for you or you may find a local genealogical society in the area of your desired research. You may rent books or microfilm to use at home or you may have access to a Family History Center, which can borrow microfilm copies of the records you need [see chapter 4 for more information on Family History Centers]. Networks of genealogists who are Internet users often exchange research services.

Professional research can be expensive. You usually pay the researcher by the hour, plus costs of photocopies, postage, and other expenses. Although the hourly fee can be as low as $8 per hour, an average hourly fee is $15-$40. Remember, however, you may only need three or four hours of a professional's time to accomplish a specific goal.

Finding a professional researcher is a lot like finding a mechanic to work on your car: there are good and bad ones and all kinds in between. Anyone can hang out a shingle and call herself an auto mechanic—or a professional researcher. You have to be selective and use common sense. Try to find a researcher who lives near or regularly travels to the geographic area from which you need records. Generally, hiring a researcher in Salt Lake City to research original Georgia records is not the best use of your research dollars. If that researcher has access to the materials on microfilm, so do you.

To find prospective professional researchers, you can:

- Write to the state archives (or any large genealogical library) in the state in which you need research done and ask for recommendations.

- Write to the state or county genealogical or historical society in the area and ask for recommendations.

- Write to the county courthouse in the area and ask for recommendations.

- Read queries and locate other researchers who are working on families in the same geographic area where you need assistance. Write them and ask for recommendations about professionals they have hired.

- Read advertisements and the annual listing of professional researchers in *The Genealogical Helper* or other similar genealogical periodicals.

- Write the Board for Certification of Genealogists, PO Box 14291, Washington, DC 20044, and request information about how to learn who the certified researchers are in the area you need.

- Write the Association of Professional Genealogists, PO Box 40393, Denver CO 80204, and ask about purchasing a copy of their *Directory of Professional Genealogists*.

- Write the Family History Library, 35 North West Temple Street, Salt Lake City, UT 84150, and ask for their list of Accredited Genealogists.

There are pitfalls in the suggestions listed above. Because a professional has credentials from the Board for Certification of Genealogists or the Family History Library does not mean they will do a satisfactory job for you. It does mean they have passed proficiency tests in various aspects of genealogy. And it means you have some agency to complain to if you do not obtain satisfactory results from the researcher's efforts. Many excellent professional genealogists are *not* certified *or* accredited.

Because a researcher's name is listed on printed materials from libraries, archives, or genealogy societies does not ensure they will satisfactorily perform the work you need. People who place ads advertising research services in genealogical periodicals have only demonstrated they paid the money for the ad. Membership in the Association of Professional Genealogists does not automatically mean the researcher is competent, but again, if something goes wrong in the researcher-client relationship, APG does offer an arbitration service.

Personal recommendations from satisfied customers is a safe, but not foolproof, way to find a researcher.

Once you have made a list of two or three likely candidates to hire, write a short letter briefly explaining your research problem and request information about their methods, rates and turn-around time. Send the same letter to each of the researchers and enclose a SASE (self-addressed, stamped envelope). Be clear in your initial letter that you are not requesting services, just seeking information to be able to hire the work you require.

When you receive replies from the professional researchers you've written to, analyze each with a critical eye. Is the reply handwritten and difficult to decipher? Are there misspelled words or misused grammar? Does the researcher seem to have a grasp of your problem and appear capable of accomplishing your objectives? Make your decision about which person to hire based on your findings.

Once you hire a researcher, you should expect the following:

- Complete citations of all sources checked by the researcher, whether something was found in that source or not.

- A report in a timely fashion. Some good genealogists have a heavy caseload. You may have to wait months for your work to be completed, but you should be accurately advised in advance about the delay.

- A report that covers everything found, in a clear and concise manner, and an analysis of that information.
- Suggestions for further research.
- A bill within the limits set by you.

Your responsibilities are to give the researcher complete details, covering everything you know and a list of sources you have already searched for the family in question. If you do not tell them you have already searched the 1900 census and what you found, you have no basis for being angry when you are charged for the researcher to search it. On the other hand, when you tell the professional you have searched a particular source, they assume you have done a thorough search and not missed anything.

State your objectives and/or what you want searched (if you have specific records in mind). You may simply ask the researcher to find anything she can about your family.

Say how many hours of work should be done or what amount of money you will spend; remember the analysis and report time, which can be considerable, is also charged at the researcher's hourly rate.

Most people do not contract for hundreds of dollars of research at one time; they request a few hours, read the report when it arrives, then decide whether or not to continue for a few more hours, either at that time or at some later date.

Learning More

The purpose of this book has been to introduce you to genealogy and family history. You will want to read many of the books and publications suggested in the bibliography and resource sections of this book and learn more about research. For help in designing your self-directed learning experience, read Ronald Gross's *The Independent Scholar's Handbook*.

Besides your self-directed study, there are formal programs to help you learn to be a better genealogist and family historian.

- Institute of Genealogical Studies, PO Box 25556, Dallas, TX 75225, offers a week-long series of classes each year in July. The atmosphere is like a magical summer camp for genealogists. IGS is supported by Dallas Genealogical Society. Write and request that your name be put on the list to be sent a brochure about the upcoming event.

- Samford University in Birmingham, Alabama, holds the week-long Institute of Genealogy and Historical Research each year in June. Write Samford University Library, 800 Lakeshore Drive, Birmingham, AL 35229, and request a brochure.

- The National Institute on Genealogical Research is held every summer at the National Archives in Washington, DC. The week-long course provides extensive education about federal sources for experienced researchers. Write National Institute on Genealogical Research, PO Box 14274, Washington, DC 20044-4274 and request a brochure.

- Brigham Young University in Provo, Utah, offers two programs in genealogy, an associate degree and certificate program. Most of the required classes are available by correspondence. Write Brigham Young University, Department of Independent Study, 206 Harman Building, Provo, UT 84602; request a catalog.

- National Genealogical Society has a home study course for beginners, *American Genealogy: A Basic Course*. NGS holds an annual conference in a different US city, featuring intensive lecture programs. Write National Genealogical Society, 4527 17th Street North, Arlington, VA 22207-2363 for more information.

- The Federation of Genealogical Societies sponsors an annual conference in a different US city. Write FGS, PO Box 830220, Richardson, TX 75083, and ask to receive information about the next upcoming event.

- Even if you cannot travel to the NGS or FGS conferences, you can purchase cassette tape recordings of many of the lectures from Repeat Performance, 2911 Crabapple Lane, Hobart, IN 46342. Write and ask for catalogs of their genealogy conference tapes.

- As genealogy increases in popularity, some colleges are offering courses through non-credit classes. Many genealogical and historical societies hold classes and seminars on genealogy. Check events listings in genealogical periodicals.

- Don't limit your genealogical education to courses labeled "genealogy." Consider the following:
  ✓ Attend a title abstracting workshop: inquire about classes like this from the board in your state that licenses title abstracters.

✓ Ask at a local college about auditing classes in history, geography, architecture, and anthropology for the areas and time periods of your interest.

✓ Contact companies who offer career enhancement courses in business writing, communication skills, and computer use.

✓ Sign up for classes in photo and document preservation offered by local museums.

✓ Take a non-fiction writing class.

✓ Enroll in a handwriting analysis class.

✓ Visit a fortune teller and ask about the *past* instead of the *future*. (Oops, we're getting a little carried away here.)

You have taken the first step by using this book to learn how to successfully research your family history. Continue to learn about the geographic areas of your interest, other sources of information, and historical events that had an effect on your ancestors.

The Genealogical Consumer

A word of caution needs to be extended to beginning researchers about individuals and companies selling books, services and materials to genealogical consumers. Everyone *isn't* out to help you—some only seek to make a profit for themselves. Especially as a beginner, be very cautious in spending your research dollars. Use library resources whenever possible and refrain from buying books until you are certain they will be of *continuing* use to you. When you identify specific counties where your ancestors lived for extended periods, you may want to seek out and buy published secondary sources such as census transcriptions, marriage records indexes, printed tax lists and the local society's newsletter or journal. Remember to use secondary sources to find primary sources.

Advertisements that come in the mail offering you a "Complete history of the (Your Name Here) Family" are usually just what they seem: too good to be true. Save your money. Ask experienced researchers for advice about buying books. Read book reviews in major genealogical publications. Learn which reviews are critical reviews (like those in the *National Genealogical Society Quarterly* which point out both good and bad features) and which are merely non-critical "notices" (like those in *The Genealogical Helper*). Don't assume because a book is published by a major genealogical publishing company that it is accurate. Spend wisely.

Be careful about contracting for research services. Read the previous section on hiring a professional.

13 - Computers for Genealogists

Computers are useful tools for genealogists and family historians to manage a database of ancestors, write letters, and compile a family narrative. When connected to the Internet, a world-wide computer information network, computers enable genealogists to communicate with other researchers and explore a vast variety of resources.

Technology in the computer field is moving at a rapid pace; machines are getting better, faster, and less expensive. Internet access is widely available through a variety of service providers.

Choosing a Computer and Software

If you are thinking of buying a computer, talk with others who use computers and get recommendations about hardware (machinery) and software (programs that run the machinery). Contact computer interest groups in your area and use members' expertise to avoid purchasing unusual, outmoded, or unreliable equipment. Read critical reviews in computer magazines. Take non-credit computer classes at a local adult education center or community college to learn how to manage the operating system or get the most from a word processing program. Most computers sold today are equipped with CD-ROM drives and modems, essentials for genealogists.

There are many excellent commercial genealogy programs on the market. You can learn about these by reading reviews in genealogy magazines and talking with users at genealogy meetings. Programs today let you input, organize, and analyze your family data, and print it in a variety of formats. Many programs are designed for the Windows operating system, an easy-to-use, point-and-click system. Some programs let you input source citations for each bit of data, much like the paper family group sheet system we recommend. Many let you attach image files of scanned photographs.

When you ask for recommendations about software, listen carefully to what other users tell you. Is the program they're telling you about the *only* one they've used? If so, you need additional insight from other users of a variety of programs. It's hard to be certain a program meets *your* needs until you've actually begun to enter your family information. Don't ask to "borrow" a copy of a friend's software to install on your computer—it violates copyright restrictions. Instead, ask your friend for an extensive demonstration on her computer.

Though we're reluctant to choose any computer program as the *best* one on the market (because there are many great ones out there), we can tell you we've used *Family Tree Creator* by Mindscape and it does everything we've wished for. Formerly, our choice of computer programs was Personal Ancestral File (PAF) published by the LDS Church. It remains an excellent choice and has a wide user base.

The kind of computer you have will influence your software choices. You can run PAF on an antique computer with only two disk drives and no hard disk. Many businesses and individuals buy new computer equipment regularly—if you're the happy recipient of some discarded equipment, you can certainly use it for your genealogy project, but you'll be limited in the software you can run. But be very careful about buying used equipment. Computer equipment wears out and becomes outmoded very quickly and loses its value. Don't invest even a few hundred dollars unless you have some assurance used equipment will be useful to you.

When you select a modem, that device that connects your computer to your phone line, buy only the fastest speed on the market at the time of your purchase. Most new computers sold today include a modem, but ask for advice—you will save time and money with the fastest modem available. Modem speed refers to the rate at which data is transmitted through your telephone line and the faster the modem, the more quickly the transmission occurs.

A lot of computer software and genealogy information is distributed on CD-ROM (a storage medium that looks just like the compact disks music is distributed on), and if you're buying a new computer, a CD-ROM data drive will probably be included. You can add a CD-ROM drive to an older computer, though when you start upgrading older computer equipment, it's much like deciding whether to make repairs to a used car or buy a new one. Every situation is different. All information you'll find on CD-ROM isn't accurate or complete just as books aren't always accurate or complete. We're seeing a trend toward providing actual document images, instead of just indexes, in the CD-ROM format.

Consider adding a color scanner to your computer equipment. You can add photographic images to your genealogy database and copies of actual documents. These images, stored as computer files, can be transmitted as attachments to your e-mail messages. Or you can mail an album of pictures on a computer disk if your recipient doesn't have the ability to receive electronic messages.

Accessing the Internet

Newspapers and magazines are filled with stories about the Internet, the "information highway." There's truly an amazing burst of interest and for good reason. Using the Internet, you can search a library catalog in Scotland, exchange photo image files with a cousin in Austria, and participate in a discussion with hundreds of people from all over the world. How do you get involved?

First, obviously, you need a computer. Your local library may offer Internet access. If you aren't a computer owner and don't want to invest in equipment, explore your library's resources. In addition to possible Internet access, you'll find a vast amount of library resources available on CD-ROM.

If you use your own computer to access the Internet, you'll need a modem and an account with an Internet service provider or an online service. Internet service providers usually offer some basic software programs and instructions for coordinating your computer and modem with their equipment. Online services such as America Online, Prodigy, CompuServe, and others offer more features than just an Internet connection. They're often easier to configure than the programs provided by a service provider, but sometimes they're more expensive. If you're a student or teacher in any educational institution, check with your computer department to see if they offer Internet access. Online services and service providers can provide information about their billing plans. Generally, they charge a monthly fee for a certain number of basic usage hours, plus additional fees for extra hours and special services.

Your selection of an Internet access provider may depend on the availability of a local access phone number for your connection. If you live in a rural area where services like America Online don't offer a local phone number, be sure to figure some steep long distance phone bills into your budget. Or make inquiries about an Internet service provider who offers a local phone number for your connection. When your computer actually accesses the Internet, your phone line will be busy, so you may want to look into adding a second phone line.

Once you have established a way to access the Internet, the best way to learn about it is to jump in with both feet and use it! The portion of the Internet most widely used is the World Wide Web. Libraries, archives, commercial firms, historical and genealogical societies, family organizations, and just plain folks are establishing information sites called web pages. You can use search programs on the Internet to discover web pages of interest. Web pages often offer links to pages on related topics.

Much of the information on the web is commercial in nature—it's an advertising medium. Many of the sites, however, offer searches of indexes. You can search the Illinois land patent database, the Kentucky death record index, or the Texas Confederate pension index, for example. You can view maps and photographs. You can find cousins by using a database containing all the telephone directory listings for the United States. You can locate hard-to-find books.

There are discussion groups for every imaginable subject, including several for genealogists. Discussion groups, called news groups, can be a good resource if you have a question for which you can't find an answer. They're also a good place to post queries.

A Note of Caution

While the Internet is a wonderful communication avenue, there are drawbacks. Most of the resources widely available now on the Internet are secondary or compiled sources. Only a few sites offer access to images of original materials themselves. Anytime you are using compiled sources, you must remember they vary in their degree of accuracy and completeness. Just because you don't find something in an index doesn't mean it wasn't in the original source. It's easy to get caught up in the speed and ease of electronic research and leave our standards behind.

One of the biggest temptations in computer genealogy is the acquisition of "instant ancestors." When you find a distant cousin working on your family lines and that person has keyed the material into a genealogy database, it's a simple matter to transfer the information to *your* database. And with that transfer, you get "instant ancestors." But how do you know your cousin verified every link in every generation and correctly evaluated all the evidence? Resist the temptation! When you're offered electronic information, treat it just as you would data from traditional sources. Carefully cite the source *you* received it from and evaluate every new source of information and reevaluate every conclusion.

Tommy Moffitt, GEDCOM *file from PAF version 2.3 of descendants of Nathan Moffitt. 15 January 1996. Supplied on disk. Copy in file.*

Keep the information separate from the other information you've collected. If you choose to add selected portions to your family group sheets, be sure you cite to the source you took them from, not the sources cited by the person who gave the information to you. If on the other hand, you use the information to obtain the original sources and examine them yourself, you can then cite to those original sources.

As you participate in news groups' discussions on the Internet and receive e-mail messages from other researchers, you'll often find sources unmentioned. Ask for more information (in a polite, non-threatening manner, of course). And remember your citation is to the source you received—the e-mail communication or news group posting.

Computer information is mostly stored on magnetic media. Disks, both diskettes and hard drives, are subject to failure. Always make back up copies of your files. Store a set of back up copies at a different location and update them regularly.

Computers are a wonderful invention. Use them to enhance your genealogy research. Don't forget, however, the importance of using original sources, evidence evaluation, and precise citation.

Glossary

Many of the definitions given below are genealogy-specific, but most of these words have other meanings also. For more information or to look up additional legal or archaic terms, consult the *Oxford English Dictionary*, and *Black's Law Dictionary*. (Follow the cross-references in *Black's* to get the full definition.)

abstract: a written summary of the main points in a document.

abstract company: a private firm that maintains and compiles legal histories of pieces of real estate, called abstracts of title.

administrator: the court-appointed person who handles the business of a deceased person's estate, or the affairs of an incompetent person (female: administratrix).

agricultural schedule: a separate part of the federal census, listing the farmers, with statistical information about their farms and crops; 1850-1880.

allied and associated families: those families who traveled, attended church, and intermarried with and witnessed legal documents for the families being researched.

archives: a repository containing primarily the retired official records of public or private agencies.

baseline: the east-west survey line in public domain states.

bequest: specific property transferred by a will.

Bible records: vital records written in the family record pages of a Bible.

bounty land: land received from state or federal government by a veteran, his family, or an assignee, for military service.

burned county: a common term for a courthouse whose records have been lost or destroyed through fire, flood, vermin or neglect.

census: the counting or listing of inhabitants of a certain region; done by a **census enumerator** commonly on a federal or state basis.

chancery court: a court of equity; usually dealing with divorce or family matters.

Church of Jesus Christ of Latter-day Saints: commonly know as Mormons; interested in family history because of their religious beliefs.

civil lawsuits: legal cases between two or more private parties.

collateral relatives: people who share an ancestor but do not descend from one another.

compiled service record: military records that have been abstracted from various original documents, into one record, and filed alphabetically by the soldier's name.

compiled source: information abstracted from various original documents into one record; secondary source.

conflicting information: data that comes from different sources but does not agree; must be evaluated.

county court: a local jurisdiction, handling day to day business of county government.

county formation date: the creation date of a new county, either from other existing counties or from previously unorganized territory.

criminal lawsuit: legal case involving the state against one or more parties who have broken the law.

death notice: a short mention of a person's death, differentiated from an obituary by its brevity.

deed: a legal document transferring some type of property.

emigration: the act of moving from one country to another.

enumeration order: the sequence in which census entries were recorded; house to house.

estate: the property held by a person at the time of his or her death.

evidence: facts that indicate whether or not something is true; proof.

executor: the person who is named in a will to handle the affairs of an estate after the death of the deviser, (female: executrix).

extract: to copy a record, or portions of a record, verbatim from a body of records.

family group sheet: page (often a pre-printed form) listing a family unit: father, mother and children of that union, with the dates and places of birth, death and burial given for each individual, in addition to other information and source documentation.

family history: the study of the genealogy of one's family with emphasis on accumulating information on the events and circumstances of their lives, rather than mere dates, places, and lineage.

Family History Center: a genealogy library operated by the LDS Church (Mormons), where any visitor can access the extensive records amassed by the LDS Family History Library in Salt Lake City, Utah.

Family History Library: the repository of the largest collection of genealogical materials in the world; operated by the LDS Church, located in Salt Lake City, Utah; open to the public; distributes copies of microfilmed records to Family History Centers.

Family Tree Creator Deluxe: a widely-used genealogy computer program from Mindscape, Inc.

footnote: a note at the bottom of the page citing the source of or additional information about information appearing on the page; sometimes this same data appears as **endnotes**: the notes for the entire article appearing at the end of that article.

genealogical society: an organization of people associated because of their common interest in the genealogy of the families in an area (county, state, country) or an ethnic or a family group.

guardian: the person appointed by the court to oversee the interests of a minor or incompetent person; sometimes specified in a will; can be the father or mother of the minor or incompetent person.

head of household: the term used for the person whose name appears first in the census enumeration of a family or group of people living together; before 1850, the only peoples' names who appear in the census enumeration.

heirloom: an object passed down, generally within the family, from generation to generation, often of worth only due to sentimental value.

heir: a person designated by a will or by the court to receive the property of the deceased.

historical society: an organization of people associated because of their common interest in the history of an area (county, state, country).

home guard: an organized group of men in a region liable to call to arms in an emergency.

Homestead Act of 1862: law passed by the federal government setting liberal terms for the acquisition of land by people who agreed to settle on the land.

immigration: the act of moving into one country from another.

industry schedule: the additional part of the federal census detailing the business activities of those enumerated within each county; also called Products of Industry.

inter-library loan: one library borrowing, for a patron's use, books from another library system; genealogical books are often not available through inter-library loan.

intestate: without a will or a person who dies without a will.

inventory: a list of the property held by a person at the time of his death; usually compiled by several court-appointed people, who submit the list to the court for approval.

in-law: person related by marriage or by another legal tie.

irregular unit: group of armed men informally organized for a specific purpose not officially recognized by traditional army or government.

jurisdiction: the legal (or traditional) authority to carry out certain activities; political boundary within which officials have authority.

justice of the peace (JP): a local elected official with the authority to witness legal documents, perform marriages, and implement some areas of local law.

LDS: Church of Jesus Christ of Latter-Day Saints; Mormon.

legal notice: an advertisement in a newspaper fulfilling the requirements of the law for notification of other interested parties or the public.

Library of Congress: repository located in Washington, DC, originally created to serve the needs of Congress, now open to the public.

local history: the events of the past that impact a certain area; often includes family histories.

loose papers: the original legal documents (decrees, inventories, depositions, receipts, claims, petitions, etc.) usually gathered into packets as they relate to one person or action, and filed at a courthouse.

maiden name: the surname a woman is given at birth.

manuscript collection: an assortment of unpublished related papers, letters or documents, held by a library or archives, usually unindexed.

meridian: in the rectangular system, a north-south survey line.

metes and bounds: a system of land description that uses physical objects, frequently trees and rivers, and the property lines of adjacent landowners to define the boundaries of land; measurements frequently expressed in poles, a distance of about 5 1/2 yards.

microfiche: cards made of photographic material containing reduced images of printed material; used with a special reader that illuminates and enlarges the images.

microfilm: rolls of photographic material containing reduced images of printed material; used with a special microfilm reader that illuminates and enlarges the images and allows the spool of microfilm to be rolled forward and rewound onto the spool.

militia: organized armed forces of an area subject to a call to arms in an emergency.

mortality schedule: an additional part of the federal census detailing the deaths in each family within the preceding twelve- month period.

mortgage: a document placing conditions on the sale of property; usually recorded at the county level.

NATF-80 form: a form used when submitting a request for military, military pension, or bounty land records from the National Archives.

National Archives: the United States repository for documents relating to the history and people of our country.

negative research: a search of a source that yields no information, yet reveals information of a sort by the very fact that nothing was found, and gains importance from the knowledge that the source will not have to be searched again for the same reason.

neighbors: those who appear to reside in the same vicinity as the family being researched, hence may have connections to that family; inferred from their proximity of enumeration in the census record, their listing together in a tax book, intermarriage, and various other records.

nickname: first name by which one is commonly called, differing from the formal name one was given at birth.

obituary: an announcement of a person's death, giving details which may include information about the deceased's origins, biographical data, survivors, religion, and burial information; usually both a primary and secondary source.

parent county: the county from which another county is or was formed; the county from whom land was taken to create a new county or part of a new county.

pension: a stipend provided to an elderly or disabled military veteran, or to his widow or children, upon proof of military service.

periodical: a publication produced at regular intervals, such as quarterly or monthly.

Personal Ancestral File (PAF): a widely-used genealogy computer program; available from the LDS Church.

personal property: possessions held by a person, which may include livestock, gold watches, carriages, and slaves; as opposed to real property, which refers to land.

petition: a document addressed to a government entity, making a request of some sort, signed by a group of people who agree with the premise of the request.

plantation account: records kept pertaining to the business activities of a plantation, either narrative or tabular; often included vital statistics of slaves.

political boundary: the borders of a governmental jurisdiction; lines drawn on paper or maps, as opposed to physical borders.

population schedule: the main part of the federal census, listing the inhabitants (the free inhabitants, before 1870) of an area, with varying degrees of other personal data.

primary source: a record containing information recorded at or about the time of the event, as opposed to compiled or secondary information; primary sources are generally more reliable than secondary sources.

probate: the legal process by which the property of a deceased intestate individual is dispersed.

Quaker: common term for a member of the Society of Friends, a religious group noted for opposition to war and refusal to swear (they affirm instead) in legal matters.

query: an advertisement of sorts, requesting an exchange of data with readers who are interested in the history of the same family.

real property: land.

reapportionment: periodic redrawing of geographic boundaries of districts from which legislative representatives are elected; a primary purpose of early census enumeration.

rectangular survey system: a grid-like system of land division based on lines surveyed from baselines (east-west lines) and meridians (north-south lines); in use in public-land states.

regular soldier: military man serving a proscribed tour of duty in the standing army, as opposed to volunteer soldiers, those called upon to serve in an emergency or for a specific purpose.

research calendar: a list of sources searched showing surnames sought and results.

reunion: an organized gathering of people descended from a common ancestor, bearing the same surname, or bound together by some common tie.

Revolutionary War: the American war for independence, 1776 - 1783, which involved many citizens and created a variety of records helpful to genealogists.

SASE: self-addressed stamped envelope; an envelope provided to another person or correspondent by a researcher, already addressed back to that researcher and stamped with first-class postage, for the convenience of the correspondent.

secondary source: record containing information compiled long after the events discussed; generally not as reliable as a **primary** source.

slave: usually a black, mulatto, or mixed race person, bought and sold as property, kept in servitude with no individual rights.

slave schedule: an additional part of the federal census (1850 and 1860), listing the slave owners name, with a tally, by age, sex, and color, of the slaves owned by that person; no names of slaves are given.

source citation: a note, footnote or endnote, stating where the information given was derived.

superior court a court to which cases with unsatisfactory results in the eyes of either party was referred for another judgment.

surname: last name; usually the same as the surname of the father.

survey system: a plan to describe a parcel of real property (land) so ownership of it can be transferred.

tally: a counting by mark, rather than a listing by name.

tax record: list of people liable to pay taxes in a given area, with a list of their property, real and/or personal; usually compiled annually on a county level.

topographic map: map showing the physical contours of a region of land; landmarks, churches, schools, roads, and cemeteries are sometimes shown.

volunteer soldier: those called upon to serve in the armed forces in an emergency or for a specific purpose; as opposed to regular soldiers who are members of the standing armed forces; includes drafted soldiers.

War Between the States: also called the Civil War, the War of the Rebellion, or the War of Northern Aggression; fought from 1861 to 1865, between the North and the seceded Southern states.

widow's pension: the monthly or annual stipend received by a woman due to her husband's qualifying service or employment; often refers to a military pension.

will: a legal instrument directing the disposition of a person's estate, the handling of a person's affairs, and the appointment of an executor for the estate and/or a guardian for dependents after a person's death.

witness: person who signs his name to (or makes his mark on) a document, attesting to the correctness of the statements or information in the document or that the principal's signature is genuine.

Resources

Many of the non-profit and commercial firms listed below have information pages on the World Wide Web computer network. If you are an Internet user, use any of the search engines and search for the organization or company name to learn the Universal Resource Locator (URL).

The addresses and telephone numbers below are subject to change.

AGLL Genealogical Services, PO Box 329, Bountiful, UT 84011, has census and other microfilm for rental use in your home. Write, or call 800/760-AGLL, for membership information. AGLL sells a variety of books, and publishes *Heritage Quest* and *Genealogy Bulletin* magazines. Request a catalog.

Ancestry, Inc., PO Box 476, Salt Lake City, UT 84110, publishes genealogy books, forms, and a periodical, *Ancestry Magazine*. Call 800/262-3787 to request a catalog.

Association for State and Local History, 530 Church St., Suite 600, Nashville, TN 37219, publishes Directory of Historical Organizations in the United States and Canada and other books and leaflets. Write for a catalog.

Broderbund Software, Banner Blue Division, PO Box 6125, Novato, CA 94948, publishes Family Tree Maker and genealogy data on CD-ROM. Call 800/474-8696 for a catalog.

Dallas Genealogical Society, PO Box 12648, Dallas, TX 75225, sells an excellent family group sheet with space for source citation for individual data items. Write for a forms price list.

Everton Publishers, Inc., PO Box 368, Logan, UT 84321, offers a variety of books and forms for genealogists and family historians. Write, or call 800/443-6325, for a catalog. Everton publishes, among other resources, *The Handy Book for Genealogists* and *The Genealogical Helper*, a bi-monthly magazine for genealogists.

The Frontier Press, 10 Cadena Drive, Galveston, TX 77554, carries a marvelous selection of genealogical and historical books, and has an especially good collection of books on social history. Most of the books mentioned in this book are available from Frontier Press. Send a large SASE for a catalog.

Genealogical Publishing Co., Inc., 1001 N. Calvert St., Baltimore, MD 21202, publishes an extensive line of genealogy books. Call 800/296-6687 to request a catalog.

Hearthstone Bookshop, 5735-A Telegraph Rd., Alexandria, VA 22303, sells a great many genealogy books. Call (toll-free) 888/960-3300 to request a catalog.

Heritage Books, Inc., 1540E Pointer Ridge Place, Bowie, MD 20716, publishes a variety of genealogy books. Write for a free catalog of genealogy books.

Mindscape, Inc., Customer Support, One Anthenaeum Street, Cambridge, MA 02142, phone: 617/761-3000, fax: 617/494-5898, e-mail: cust_serv@learningco.com, publishes *Family Tree Creator Deluxe*.

National Genealogical Society, 4527 17th Street North, Arlington, VA 22207-2363, sells a variety of forms, research aids and books. Individual membership is $40/year and includes a subscription to the National Genealogical Society Quarterly and the NGS Newsletter. NGS sells the family group sheet recommended in this book. Write and ask for a membership brochure, forms price list, and information about their home study course, American Genealogy: A Basic Course.

New England Historic Genealogical Society, 101 Newbury St., Boston, MA 02116, offers valuable member benefits for those with New England ancestors. Write for a membership application.

The Ellen Payne Odom Genealogy Library publishes a bi-monthly newspaper, The Family Tree, for researchers. It's of interest to all family historians, but carries special items about Scottish clan research. To subscribe, send a small postage donation to Odom Library, PO Box 1110, Moultrie, GA 31776.

Research Associates, an imprint of Arkansas Research, PO Box 303, Conway, AR 72033, publishes *Beginner's Guide to Family History Research*, 3rd ed. and other helpful methodology books.

Scholarly Resources, 104 Greenhill Ave., Wilmington, DE 19805, sells National Archives microfilm. Call 800/772-8937 for more information and to request a leaflet about your particular state of interest.

Bibliography

Go to your local library and inquire about these books. Ask about inter-library loan for the books your local library doesn't have. For the books you'd like to own, we've included vendor information in the Resource section of this book.

Allen, Desmond Walls. *Where to Write for Confederate Pension Records.* 2nd ed. Conway, Ark.: Research Associates, 1994. [Order from the publisher, PO Box 303, Conway, AR 72033; $5.95 postpaid.]

Allen, Desmond Walls. *Where to Write for County Maps.* 2nd ed. Conway, Ark.: Research Associates, 1995. [Order from the publisher, PO Box 303, Conway, AR 72033; $5.95 postpaid.]

Beers, Henry Putney. *The Confederacy: A Guide to the Archives of the Government of the Confederate States of America.* Washington, DC: National Archives Trust Fund Board, 1986. [See Munden for the companion Union volume.]

Billington, Ray Allen. *Westward Expansion: A History of the American Frontier.* New York: The Macmillan Co., 1949. [Subsequent editions have been published—check used bookstores and libraries.]

Boorstin, Daniel J. *The Americans: The Colonial Experience.* New York: Random House, 1958. [Paperback editions of this series are still in print.]

Boorstin, Daniel J. *The Americans: The National Experience.* New York: Random House, 1965.

Boorstin, Daniel J. *The Americans: The Democratic Experience.* New York: Random House, 1973.

Brackman, Barbara, *Clues in the Calico: Identifying and Dating Quilts*, McLean, VA: EPM Publications, Inc., 1989. [Order from the publisher, PO Box 490, McLean, VA 22101; price $39.95 plus $3.00 postage.]

Carpenter, Cecelia Svinth, *How to Research American Indian Blood Lines: A Manual on Indian Genealogical Research* Orting, WA: Heritage Quest, 1987.

The Chicago Manual of Style, Fourteenth Edition, Chicago: University of Chicago Press, 1993.

Clegg, Michael B. and Curt B. Witcher. *PERiodical Source Index.* Fort Wayne, Ind.: Allen County Public Library Foundation, 1986+. [Indexes most genealogical periodicals in annual volumes; retrospective series, 1847-1985, in production.]

Colletta, John Phillip. *They Came in Ships: A Guide to Finding Your Immigrant Ancestor's Arrival Record.* Revised ed. Salt Lake City, Utah: Ancestry, 1993.

Dick, Everett. *The Dixie Frontier: A Social History.* Norman, Okla.: University of Oklahoma Press, 1993.

Dollarhide, William. *Managing a Genealogical Project.* Revised Ed. Baltimore, Md.: Genealogical Publishing Co., 1996.

Eakle, Arlene and Johni Cerny, eds. *The Source: A Guidebook of American Genealogy,* Salt Lake City, UT: Ancestry Publishing, 1984. [Revised edition due for 1997 publication.]

Federation of Genealogical Societies. *Federation of Genealogical Societies 1996 Membership Directory.* Richardson, Texas: the Federation, 1996. [Write FGS, PO Box 830220, Richardson, TX 75083, and ask about the most recent edition.]

Fischer, David Hackett. *Albion's Seed: Four British Folkways in America.* New York: Oxford University Press, 1989.

Gates, Paul W. *History of the Public Land Law Development.* New York: Public Land Law Development Commission, 1968.

Gowers, Sir Ernest, *The Complete Plain Words,* revised by Sidney Greenbaum and Janet Whitcut, Boston: David R. Godine, Publisher, Inc., 1988. [Great resource for writers with a tendency toward verbosity.]

Greenwood, Val D., *The Researcher's Guide to American Genealogy* Second Edition, Baltimore, Md.: Genealogical Publishing Company, 1990.

Groene, Bertram Hawthorne, *Tracing Your Civil War Ancestor,* New York: Ballantine Books, 1973. [Useful for searches about artifacts; not especially helpful on identifying soldiers.]

Gross, Ronald. *The Independent Scholar's Handbook.* Berkeley, Calif.: Ten Speed Press, 1993. [Applicable to any self-directed learning project.]

Guide to Genealogical Research in the National Archives. Washington, DC: National Archives Trust Fund Board, 1985.

Guide to the National Archives of the United States. Washington, DC: National Archives Trust Fund Board, 1987.

Gutman, Herbert G., *The Black Family in Slavery and Freedom 1750-1925*, New York: Vintage Books, 1976.

The Handy Book. 8th ed. Logan, Utah: Everton Publishers, 1991.

Hatcher, Patricia Law. *Producing a Quality Family History.* Salt Lake City, Utah: Ancestry, 1996.

Higgins, J.S. *Subdivisions of the Public Lands.* 1894 reprint. Conway, Ark.: Arkansas Research, 1996. [Textbook on learning the survey system. Order from the publisher, PO Box 303, Conway, AR 72033; $25.00 plus $3.00 postage.]

Hoffman, Marian, ed. *Genealogical & Local History Books in Print.* 5th ed. Baltimore, Md.: Genealogical Publishing Co., 1996. [Continues Netti Schreiner-Yantis' series.]

Index to Personal Names in the National Union Catalog of Manuscript Collections, 1959-1984. Alexandria, Va.: Chadwyck-Healy, Inc., 1988.

Kaminkow, Marion J. *Genealogies in the Library of Congress: A Bibliography of Family Histories in America and Great Britain.* 3 vols. Baltimore, Md.: Magna Carta Co., 1974. [Supplements to this series were published in 1977 and 1987.]

Kaminkow, Marion J. *United States Local Histories in the Library of Congress.* 5 vols. Baltimore, Md.: Magna Carta Co., 1975-1976.

Kirkham, E. Kay. *How to Read the Handwriting and Records of Early America.* Salt Lake City, Utah: Kay Publishing Co., 1961. [Reprinted by Everton Publishers.]

Lackey, Richard, *Cite Your Sources: A Manual for Documenting Family Histories and Genealogical Records*, Jackson, MS: University Press of Mississippi, 1980.

Lainhart, Ann S. *State Census Records.* Baltimore, Md.: Genealogical Publishing Co., 1992.

Light, Sally. *House Histories: A Guide to Tracing the Genealogy of Your Home.* Spencertown, New York: Golden Hill Press, Inc., 1993.

McAlester, Virginia and Lee McAlester. *A Field Guide to American Houses.* New York: Alfred A. Knopf, 1995.

Merrill, Boynton Jr. *Jefferson's Nephews: A Frontier Tragedy*. 2nd ed. Louisville, Ky: The University of Kentucky Press, 1987.

Meyer, Mary K., ed. *Meyer's Directory of Genealogical Societies in the USA and Canada 1994*. Mt. Airy, Md.: Libra Publications, 1994. [Inquire about more recent editions. Libra Publications, 5179 Perry Road, Mt. Airy, MD 21771.]

Mills, Elizabeth Shown. *Evidence! Citation and Analysis for the Family Historian*. Publication information not set, 1997.

Morgan, Ted. *A Shovel of Stars: The Making of the American West 1800 to the Present*. New York: Simon and Schuster, 1995.

Morgan, Ted. *Wilderness at Dawn: The Settling of the North American Continent*. New York: Simon and Schuster, 1993.

Munden, Kenneth W. and Henry Putney Beers. *The Union: A Guide to Federal Archives Relating to the Civil War*. Washington, DC: National Archives Trust Fund Board, 1986. [See Beers for the companion Confederate volume.]

National Union Catalog of Manuscript Collections. 29 vols. Washington, DC: Library of Congress, 1959-1993. [See *Index to Personal Names in the National Union Catalog of Manuscript Collections*.]

Neagles, James C. *Confederate Research Sources: A Guide to Archive Collections*. Salt Lake City, Utah: Ancestry, 1986.

Oberly, James W. *Sixty Million Acres: American Veterans and the Public Lands Before the Civil War*. Kent, Ohio: Kent State University Press, 1990.

Parker, J. Carlyle. *Going to Salt Lake City to do Family History Research*, Turlock, Calif.: Marietta Publishing Co., 1989. [Order from the publisher at 2115 N. Denair Avenue, Turlock, CA 95380; price $10.95 plus $1.50 postage. See also the Warrens on the same subject.]

Schreiner-Yantis, Netti, ed. *Genealogical & Local History Books in Print*. 4th edition plus supplements. Maine, New York: GBIP - New York Branch, 1992. [See Hoffman, Marian for the latest edition.]

Shull, Wilma Sadler. *Photographing Your Heritage*. Salt Lake City, Utah: Ancestry Publishing, 1989.

Shumway, Gary L. and William G. Hartley. *An Oral History Primer*. Salt Lake City, Utah: the authors, 1983.

Stevenson, Noel C. *Genealogical Evidence: A Guide to the Standard of Proof Relating to Pedigrees, Ancestry, Heirship and Family*

History. Revised Ed. Laguna Hills, Calif.: Aegean Park Press, 1989.

Thorndale, William, and William Dollarhide. Map Guide to the US Federal Censuses, 1790-1920. Baltimore, Md.: Genealogical Publishing Co., 1987.

Towle, Laird C. *Genealogical Periodical Annual Index.* Bowie, Md.: Heritage Books, Inc., 1962 -. [See also PERsi.]

United States Department of Health and Human Services. *Where to Write for Vital Records: Births, Deaths, Marriages and Divorces.* Washington, DC: Government Printing Office, 1993.

US Department of Commerce, Bureau of Census. *Twenty Censuses: Population and Housing Questions, 1790-1980.* Washington, DC: Government Printing Office, 1979.

Warren, Paula Stuart and James W. Warren. *Getting the Most Mileage from Genealogical Research Trips.* 2nd ed. St. Paul, Minn.: Warren Research and Publishing, 1993. [Updated version planned for 1997. Order from the publisher, 1869 Laurel Ave., St. Paul, MN 55104; $8.00 plus $1.75 postage.]

Warren, Paula Stuart and James W. Warren. *Making the Most of Your Research Trip to Salt Lake City.* 5th ed. St. Paul, Minn.: Warren Research and Publishing, 1996. [Order from the publisher, 1869 Laurel Ave., St. Paul, MN 55104; $8.00 plus $1.75 postage.]

Wright, Norman E. *Preserving Your American Heritage.* Provo, Utah: Brigham Young University Press, 1981.

Zinsser, William, *On Writing Well: An Informal Guide to Writing Nonfiction*, 3rd edition, New York: Harper and Row, 1985. [Essential for writers of family history.]

Index

D

E

F

G

H

I

J

K

L

M

N

About the Authors

Desmond Walls Allen

Desmond Walls Allen is a publisher of Arkansas resource materials; owner of Arkansas Research, a research and publishing company; guest expert in episode one of the PBS *Ancestors* television series; past-president and board member of Arkansas Genealogical Society; co-founder and secretary-treasurer of Professional Genealogists of Arkansas; editor of *Arkansas Historical and Genealogical Magazine*; genealogy columnist for *The Times* newspaper in Shreveport; member of National Genealogical Society and former chairman of the NGS Instructor Development Committee; member of Arkansas Historical Association; past trustee for the Association of Professional Genealogists and awarded APG's Grahame Thomas Smallwood Jr. Award of Merit in 1993; awarded the Federation of Genealogical Societies' Distinguished Service Award in 1994; awarded Dallas Genealogical Society's Distinguished Service Award in 1995; author/compiler of 157 books and many articles about Arkansas historical materials; teacher and lecturer for genealogical workshops and seminars; problem-solving course coordinator, Genealogical Institute of Texas (1993, 1994, 1995) and Institute of Genealogical Studies (1996); lecturer at NGS and FGS Conferences; graduate of Samford University's Institute of Genealogy and Historical Research, "Advanced Methodology" 1988, "Genealogy as a Profession" 1989, and "America's Wars" 1991; graduate of National Institute on Genealogical Research 1990; graduate (magna cum laude) of University of Arkansas at Little Rock (BSE); holds a master's degree in history; member of Phi Kappa Phi Honor Society and Mensa, the international organization for individuals with IQ's at or above the 98th percentile.

Carolyn Earle Billingsley

Carolyn Earle Billingsley is a professional genealogist with many years experience; past editor (five years) of *The Saline*, the quarterly publication of the Saline County History and Heritage Society, Inc., of whom she is a founding member and an officer; past-president and former board member of Arkansas Genealogical Society; author of seven genealogical books; teacher and lecturer for genealogical workshops and seminars; listed in *Who's Who in Genealogy and Heraldry* 1990, and *Who's Who Among College Students* 1993-1994; co-founder of Professional Genealogists of Arkansas; past co-editor of *Professional Genealogists of Arkansas Newsletter*; member of National Genealogical Society, Arkansas Historical Association and the Association of Professional Genealogists; graduate of Samford University's Institute of Genealogy and Historical Research, "Genealogy as a Profession" 1989; graduate (summa cum laude) University of Arkansas at Little Rock (BA, History); member Phi Alpha Theta and Phi Kappa Phi; recipient of a Fulbright Scholarship for graduate work in Graz, Austria; currently completing the requirements for a Ph.D. in history at Rice University in Houston.